Operation Dynamo

About the Author

Jean Daish was born in Leeds and is the wife of a retired Royal Air Force officer. Along with their son and daughter, the family became used to moving throughout the United Kingdom and overseas. Cornwall was home for several years.

Inspired by the birth of the first of her four grandchildren twenty years ago, Jean attended a writing course and began writing short stories, articles and poetry for children and teenagers.

Operation Pied Piper, her first book, was published in 2013 and *Operation Dynamo*, featuring the same children, is the sequel.

Following twenty-seven house moves during their time with the RAF, Jean and her husband are now settled in their home county of Yorkshire.

Operation Dynamo

Operation Dynamo

Written and Illustrated by Jean Daish

Olympia Publishers
London

www.olympiapublishers.com
OLYMPIA PAPERBACK EDITION

A CIP catalogue record for this title is
available from the British Library.

ISBN: 978-1-84897-747-1

First Published in 2016

Olympia Publishers
60 Cannon Street
London
EC4N 6NP

Printed in Great Britain

Dedication

Operation Dynamo and *Operation Pied Piper* are dedicated to the evacuees separated from their families during World War II and to their carers both in the United Kingdom and overseas.

Acknowledgments

My thanks, firstly, to Olympia Publishers in all departments for their encouragement and guidance during the publication of both *Operation Pied Piper* and *Operation Dynamo*.

My thanks to friend Helen Webster for her professional presentation, typing and enthusiasm.

Thank you to my four wonderful grandchildren who continue to inspire me.

Last, but not least, a big thank you to my husband John who has guided me through some involved but satisfying research.

Prologue

Operation Dynamo took its name from the Dynamo Room in the Naval Headquarters below Dover Castle, which contained the dynamo, which provided the building with electricity during World War II. It was in this room that Vice-Admiral Bertram Ramsey planned operations and briefed Prime Minister Winston Churchill on the progress of the operation.

Chapter One

Vera yawned, stretching her skinny arms above her head and turned to face me.

"Right, then. What we goin' to do now we've won the war?"

Barely awake, I couldn't think for a moment what on earth Vera meant.

"Hardly won the war, Vera - just did our bit!" I answered over the bedsheet.

"Don't let it go to your head, Vera."

"Go to my head!"

Vera jumped out of bed, sniffed loudly (she always did that when excited) and threw her pillow at me.

"We caught two spies, helped to rescue Billy and Jack from that evil housekeeper at Gull House, saved Mrs Cadel from some terrible fate and drove away a U-boat from Cornish shores. I don't think I'm letting anything go to my head - sorry, our heads."

"It was pretty exciting and exhausting and frightening, Vera, but we have to carry on now. You know what has to be done next."

"No - what?" said Vera, struggling into her shorts and making a pathetic attempt at brushing her unruly hair.

"We have to prepare for our scholarship exams."

"What! But I'm a dunce, I can't - I'll be sick!"

"Don't be silly, Vera - you are not a dunce and I will help you prepare. We have to do it, so there is no use arguing."

Vera slumped onto her bed.

"But what happens if you pass and I fail - we'll 'ave to go to different schools, Pol."

"Let's just see, shall we? Come on, Vera - time for breakfast."

In fact, the thought of going to a different school and being away from Padstow without Vera filled me with dread. Since the excitement of last autumn and our celebrity status, Vera's confidence had grown and we had both gained new friendships. We had come to love Padstow School and life with Denzil and Ma Trewithen. They were taking care of us like they would their own family, instead of evacuees from Yorkshire.

Chapter Two

Instead of the harsh and bitter Yorkshire winter, the Cornish one was filled with barmy days except for the occasional low mists and rolling waves.

Aunt Jean had said I would enjoy the softer climate, and I was much healthier. Vera enjoyed robust health and the painfully skinny arms and legs had plumped out. Well, almost. Dear Aunt Jean, on her own in Leeds with Trouble the cat, was having difficulty keeping the little sweet and tobacconist shop going since the rationing restrictions. But her letters were always cheery.

"Girls - how about doing some musseling for us?" Ma Trewithen called from the yard.

"Denzil is down with the boat, and Billy and Jack are helping him scrape the bottom ready for the spring."

The thought of mussels for tea cooked in Ma's homemade elderberry wine filled us with instant enthusiasm.

"You'll need your jumpers - that wind is still cool, but it will be nice down on the beach - put roses in your cheeks, it will."

Ma was obsessed with rosy cheeks.

Weekends from school were heaven. Vera and I pottered about Quay Cottage helping Ma with the chores and feeding the hens, and the boys loved going on the boat with Denzil. Jack had decided he was definitely going to be a coastguard when he grew up. He and Billy hardly ever mentioned Leeds, their home or their Gran, Mum and Dad. And they never talked of their time at Gull House.

Padstow was buzzing with people. Babies were being wheeled in vast prams, and older children threw stale bread to the ever present gulls wheeling and swooping close to the prams, whilst anxious mothers flapped their arms to shoo them away.

Vera and I waved to Denzil and the boys as we passed them on the receding tide, carrying our buckets. We only had an hour before the tide turned. Denzil's fishing boat was sitting high on a trolley out of the water and he and the boys were heads down, scraping the barnacles off the bottom of Morwenna, as the boat was called.

Vera sang at the top of her voice as we walked the beach towards the rocks where we would find the mussels. Above, the windows of Gull House, which dominated the cliff top, twinkled in the low sun. We had no fear of Gull House now. But that's a different story.

"Come on, slowcoach."

Vera, swinging her bucket, prised the mussels from the rocks with her spade.

"Coming, Vera - coming." I ran now to catch up with my friend. And then I saw it - lying just ahead of me between the rocks. A crumpled sack or suchlike and, as I drew closer, it moved.

"Vera, come quick, I've found something," I shouted across the beach.

"Polly - you open it - I don't like the look of it."

The bag was wet, almost submerged in a rock pool and the string tying it together was difficult to budge.

"Hurry up, Pol!"

The bag made a sound. We looked at one another and quickly untied the knots together, our hands trembling.

"Well - look at that, Polly."

First a black nose, followed by a ragged ear and, finally, a sodden, sad little face appeared.

"It's a dog! A puppy." Vera whispered in wonder.

In a second, she had shed her jumper and was wrapping the tiny shivering form in it, and clasping it to her scrawny chest.

"How? Who?" Vera spluttered. "Polly, who would do such a thing?" The tears fell onto the already sodden head of the puppy.

"Quick, Vera, let's get it back to Ma - she will know what to do."

Denzil and the boys didn't notice us racing across the beach towards Quay Cottage with our precious bundle.

Chapter Three

What make is it Denzil?

"Is it a boy or a girl?" Billy peered over the box on the wooden range.

"You mean, is it a dog or a bitch, Billy," corrected Denzil, his enormous hands cosying the puppy in the towel. "It's a bitch, a small one at that."

"What make is it?" enquired Jack.

"You mean what breed, Jack. Difficult to say, she's so tiny. Maybe a Jack Russell or some other terrier. She's obviously the runt of the litter."

"What's a runt, Denzil?" asked Billy, pushing Jack aside to take a closer look at the sleeping pup.

"The weakest and the smallest. She may not survive, boys, but we will do our best." More warmed milk was coaxed into the puppy's mouth.

"Almost time for school, boys, finish your breakfast."

"Is it alright, Ma?" Vera peeped at the sleeping puppy, milk dribbling from the corner of its mouth.

"It's a she, Vera," said Ma.

"A girl dog, that's lovely! We can keep her, can't we Ma?"

"As long as she learns not to chase my hens, I don't see why not." Vera wrapped her arms around Ma's waist and I, looking on, saw the glistening in Ma's eyes.

"Now stop this nonsense and scoot!"

"What shall we call her, Polly?" Vera trotted alongside me across the Quay.

"I suppose we should take a vote. We'll get everyone to put their suggestions in a box and we'll pull one out."

The school day seemed endless, and seeing Billy and Jack at dinner time we told them the plan.

At least the excitement had taken our minds off the exam that Vera and I would take at the end of the week.

"'Lucky!' That's a grand name, just right." said Vera as Ma's slip of paper was pulled out of the box.

"Well, she is lucky that you girls found the bag."

"But I wanted to call her Mabel," sulked Billy.

Vera and I didn't sleep very well the night before our exam. We lay chatting in bed about the events of last year when we were so deeply involved with the strange events at Gull House. The boys had settled in so well with us at Quay Cottage it was hard to believe that they had ever stayed there.

"I've got Cornish pasties for tea, girls, to celebrate the end of your exams. Now sit down and tell me how it went!" Ma put the steaming pasties on the table, folded her arms and listened intently.

"Well - wwwell," spluttered Vera. "I answered all the questions but I don't know if they were the right ones!"

"And you, Polly, how did you get on?"

"Me too - answered everything but almost ran out of time."

"Well, it's over now and I'm sure you did your best. You need to write home and tell them about it. Don't forget the puppy."

After tea, Lucky was lifted from her box and placed on the kitchen floor where, on shaking her legs, she promptly did a wee. Laughter filled the kitchen as we watched Lucky find her way around Quay Cottage.

"I do believe she is going to be alright," said Ma lifting her back into her warm box and stroking her soft head.

"Have you ever had children, Ma?" Vera shocked me with her question.

"A very long time ago, Vera. Denzil and I had a little girl, but she died. I'll take you to see where she rests one day, but not now - I have washing to do!"

Chapter Four

Something was happening at Gull House.

Waking up to find Lucky nibbling my toes, I saw immediately the cliff top alive with tractors and diggers and suchlike.

"Vera, Vera, come and look." I pulled the blanket off a sleeping tousled Vera.

"Get her off!"

Lucky was licking Vera's face and struggling to get under the sheet.

"It's a bit early, isn't it?" Vera yawned.

"Come here and see! There's something going on up at Gull House. It looks as if it's being pulled down!"

"Why would they do that?" said Vera, kneeling beside me below the window as we both watched the activity high on the cliff.

"Let's get dressed quickly and go to the quay, maybe we will see someone there who can tell us."

A chill spring wind hit us as we quietly left the cottage and made for the quay front. We left Lucky yapping in frustration at not being able to join us. The house would be wide awake in no time.

Ned the fisherman was preparing his nets, ready for the first haul. He looked up and smiled.

"Morning, girls, a bit early for 'ee."

"Ned," I asked. "What's happening up at Gull House?"

"Well, I did hear it's goin' to be turned into a hotel or somethin'. Ask Denzil, girls - 'e'll know!"

And Ned turned his attention back to his nets.

"Denzil - what's happening up at Gull House?" said Vera, trying to stop Lucky from eating her shoe under the kitchen table.

"Not sure, girls. All I know is Mrs Cadel, the owner, has moved to Redruth. We'll find out in due time, news travels fast in Padstow."

Denzil wiped his beard on a spotted handkerchief, raised his considerable bulk from the table and waved goodbye.

We joined Ma in the snug, Vera and I. She sat with her head close to the wireless. "Blessed thing!" She banged the ancient wireless which made it stutter even more.

"You ready for school, girls? Bless me, Vera, 'av 'e brushed your hair?"

"Yes, Ma." Vera ran her fingers through her unruly mop. "It just won't do as it's told."

"You look worried, Ma," I asked.

Ma sighed deeply.

"Denzil's just missed the news - it's not good. Germany is building up her forces and we are doing the same. The 'phoney war' is over. Lord preserve us, what will happen next?"

Chapter Five

The blackthorn blossom came early. Every hill and field was glowing with the snow-white flowers and the gorse, yellow as custard, jostled for space.

"Too early," cautioned Ma. "Not a good sign - mark me."

Ma's mood was echoed by news both on the wireless and in the Newquay Herald's headlines the next day.

"BLITZKRIEG!"

"Norway, Denmark and Holland overrun by the Germans who are now heading for Belgium towards France."

And later that day, as we were having tea, the wireless coughed out:

"British Army sent to stop the advance are forced to retreat and are trapped between the German Army and the English Channel at Dunkirk."

Vera was inconsolable.

"My poor brother," she sobbed. "Whatever will happen to him?" Vera's brother was with the British Expeditionary Force somewhere in France.

"Now, Vera dear," said Ma, holding her close to her chest but with tears filling her eyes. "You don't think for one moment Vera that the British people would leave those poor lads alone. You see - someone will sort something out."

It didn't seem right that the sun was shining and mothers were playing on the beach with their children. It was May and it felt wrong for us to be enjoying the warm spring at all. Vera and I had forgotten all about our examination results.

Instead, we all went to Chapel where the Minister asked us to pray for our troops and that Mr Churchill, the new Prime Minister, would be supported by our prayers.

"What does Blitzkrieg mean, Denzil?" asked Billy the next day after the news bulletin.

"'Lightning strike', Billy or some such thing." Denzil stroked his red beard thoughtfully at the same time as stroking Billy's head with the other hand. "Worry not me 'andsome. We'll not let the Germans walk our beaches, you see. Now come with me and Jack. I need to check Morwenna."

"Why is it - sorry she, called Morwenna, Denzil?"

"Called after our precious little girl, Billy. She died when she was only four of whooping cough. She loved that boat she did, and she caught more mackerel than I ever did."

"What's whooping cough? I've got a cough," said Jack, forcing out a weak splutter.

"Not like your cough, Jack, you just don't like the blossom." Denzil gave Billy a giant hug, lifting him off his feet.

"I can't sleep, Pol." Vera nudged closer to me that night.

29

"I'm not surprised, Vera, I don't suppose many people will be sleeping at night just now. Try counting sheep."

"I can't - they jump too quickly."

"What's your brother's name, Vera?"

"You mustn't laugh, Polly."

"Of course not."

"It's Lionel, and he hates it. Used to get called Lionhead at school."

"But it's a lovely name - very manly."

"Eh - well he's just our kid really."

And despite the dreadful news, we giggled, holding onto one another tightly in the comfort of our shared bed.

Mr Churchill did have a plan and, although we didn't yet know it, the plan would involve Morwenna, Denzil's precious boat.

Chapter Six - The Little Ships

The atmosphere in Quay Cottage was tense, and Ma's prediction that the blackthorn blossom coming too early heralded a bad turn to the weather came true. The wind howled across the quay, making the seagulls collide with one another.

There were whisperings between Ma and Denzil, their heads close together around the kitchen table.

"Girls, Billy and Jack, come sit with us, we need to speak. Polly, put Lucky in the bedroom."

We sat white-faced around the table, Ma occasionally dabbing her eyes with the corner of her apron.

Denzil spoke. "Mr Churchill, our new Prime Minister, wants as many sailors to sail from the south coast across to Dunkirk in France, to remove our British soldiers and the French, too. They are trapped close to the Dunkirk beaches and there are lots and lots of them - thousands."

Vera jumped to her feet, flung her arms around Denzil's neck, tears coursing down her cheeks.

"Now Vera, don't fret - we'll do our best to get your brother back safe."

"I want to come, Denzil," said Billy forcefully.

"Billy, you and Jack and the girls have to stay here and look after Ma and Quay Cottage. Anyway, I need every spare inch of space in Morwenna to carry the troops."

"All right Denzil - don't worry. I'll be the man of the house when you're gone." Billy was growing up quickly.

"Good lad," Denzil beamed. "Now listen carefully," He continued. "Brian's Dad is taking the Padstow lifeboat. There'll be no fishing anyway for a while. It's risky leaving you without a reserve boat but it must be done. The Ministry is requisitioning all the lifeboats in the country and the civilian crews. Every man will do his bit. We have to sail down south first, of course, to Ramsgate or Dover and then cross the Channel. We shall have the support of the RAF, God bless them, but we have to get to Ramsgate first, and so we are leaving the day after tomorrow."

Over the evening Ma and we girls busied ourselves making dozens of Cornish pasties, wrapped and placed in one of the ice filled crates used for fish. Not much meat, but thick, filling pastry and lots of the precious veg from the garden. There were many pairs of fishermen's socks, blankets and water. Even two bottles of brandy.

"Denzil, I really want to help - what can I do tomorrow?" Billy pleaded.

"You can come help me check Morwenna, both of you boys - we need to load her up carefully, leaving maximum space. Pity the weather has turned, but we can't help that."

The cranky old wireless was on permanently now. King George VI had called for an unprecedented week of prayer.

There was a lull in the bad weather and so the flotilla changed its plan, and was to leave for Ramsgate early next day. It was thought that the sail round the coast would take two days. Denzil said there were even little ships coming down from Glasgow.

So, in the end, it was all a rush. Lucky tore about the cottage whining and yapping, knowing that something important was happening in sleepy Quay Cottage.

Early in the morning, wrapped warmly, we villagers met on Padstow beach headed by the National Lifeboat with two crew. The crew's wives and children huddled together for support and comfort.

Morwenna looked very small and vulnerable, but Denzil busied himself checking the rigging and the outboard motor, his red beard barely visible under all the warm clothing. But we saw his beaming face as he waved goodbye - Denzil the courageous fisherman doing his best for 'the lads'. He looked completely at home on Morwenna and, as we waved and Lucky yapped her goodbyes, something told us that all would be well – although we wouldn't hear any news for a long time. People prayed throughout the country for a 'miraculous delivery'. The Archbishop of Canterbury led prayers 'for soldiers in dire peril in France'. Similar prayers were said in churches and synagogues for the desperate plight of the troops. 'Operation Dynamo', as the operation was named, was imminent. And all we could do in Padstow was wait and pray.

Chapter Seven

Exhausted by our preparations for Denzil's departure, Vera and I slept in. There was the usual screeching of gulls but mostly it was the silence I noticed. Padstow was deserted.

Vera woke - scratched her mop, yawned and sat up in bed.

"I did sleep and I didn't even need to count sheep, but I dreamt I was sailing with the flotilla - so perhaps that's why I feel sick this morning." And her tousled head disappeared under the sheet again.

I left Vera dozing and climbed down to the kitchen.

"Morning, Polly - you all right, midear?"

"Yes, I'm fine, Ma - Vera says she feels sick, though."

"I expect she is anxious - about her brother. I must try and think of some way to help."

By the time we were eating breakfast, Ma had formed a plan.

"Girls - time to write home again. I don't know what the postal services will be like, but you must try. Now Vera - I might be running ahead of myself, but when you write to Mam and Dad I want to give you the telephone number of our post office.

There aren't any telephones in Padstow but there is one there. If, and I mean if, and when there is news of your brother, it will go to Mam and Dad but they can then ring the post office. It will be sometime yet though, midear - the rescue isn't underway yet. Anyway, what do you think?" But Ma knew also that if the news was bad there would be a telegram to Vera's parents.

Vera's answer was a wordless hug for Ma.

Letters were written after school that day. Polly helped Billy and Jack write a letter home. They were reluctant, but did well in the end.

"You do know your address in Leeds, don't you Billy?"

"It's No 2, Seminary Street, Leeds," answered Billy confidently.

I wrote a letter to Auntie Jean but did not, of course, mention 'the rescue'.

"Now midears, we cannot sit around the wireless all day - we'll go for a walk, maybe up the coastal path to have a nosey at Gull House. Lucky has been sulking behind the kitchen door since Denzil left. She won't eat or drink, but I think if we can get her out with us she will perk up."

Ma gave me one of Denzil's spotted handkerchiefs to put round Lucky's neck and tied a piece of string to it. She did look very cute, but a bit confused.

The view over to Rock from the coastal path was spectacular. We still hadn't been to Rock. The cliff was pretty deserted except for the occasional dog. Lucky cowered at the prospect of meeting another canine, so Vera carried her some of the way.

When we arrived at Gull House there were no workmen. The house looked abandoned and everywhere was such a mess. And then we saw Bernard, who had gardened for Mrs Cadel, the owner, when she was in residence.

"Now then Bernard, how are you midear?" enquired Ma.

"Not bad, Ma, but look at my garden or the place where my garden used to be." Bernard glared at the chaos.

"It does look a mess, Bernard; what's happening up here? I heard Gull House was being turned into a hotel."

"No Ma, the Ministry have commissioned it for use as a recovery place, not quite a hospital but somewhere our injured lads can recover their senses - poor devils. I thought I'd seen the last of wars with Germany after the last one. Silly beggars. Warring never pays."

"Well, that's very interesting, Bernard. How long before they finish?"

"Depends how many tea breaks, Ma! What have we got here then?" Bernard stroked Lucky's head.

"We found her abandoned on the beach, nearly dead," said Vera, hugging a quivering Lucky.

"Well, she fell right on her feet then, finding Quay Cottage. Or should I say paws. Ma would take a lost camel in!"

The spring air was filled with laughter.

"Come along wi' me - I've got something for 'ee."

We followed Bernard to his garden shed, where there were four rabbits strung from the roof.

"Ugh," said Billy, "that's disgusting!"

"You never tasted roasted rabbit, lad. Ma will give you a treat and that pup of yours will be very partial, I'm sure."

Jack elected to carry the rabbit back down the coastal path, making sure it didn't touch his legs. Almost home, Vera put Lucky down and she straight away ran down the path, string and spotted hanky flying, headed straight for Quay Cottage.

"Well - she knows her home." said Ma.

Once in the kitchen Lucky took up her sentry duty behind the door - and waited.

Chapter Eight

"What on earth is that racket?" Vera sat up in bed and, at the same time, Billy and Jack appeared at our bedroom door, white, faced and very rumpled.

"It's Ma, Vera - Ma is singing her favourite hymn - very loudly." I said, grabbing Vera's hand and running downstairs. A comical sight greeted us. Ma with Lucky in her arms was waltzing round the kitchen table.

"One more step along the road we go ..."

"Come on - join in!" she encouraged, and soon we were dancing through the kitchen, into the garden, round the hencoop and back again -singing along with her, still holding Lucky aloft. The gulls dipped and screeched in alarm around us.

Eventually, out of breath, red faced but grinning, Ma plonked herself down. Lucky was already back on sentry duty.

"Best get dressed, midears." she said, taking out the frying pan ready to scramble some eggs.

"Why Ma, why are you so happy?" I asked.

"Because, my darling, I just had a message down from the coastguard station. Denzil, Jimmy and Brian's Dad have reached the south coast. They sailed nonstop through 48 hours and they've arrived safely. Now they can do their job."

A great cheer went up from us, hugging one another and jumping up and down.

"Now don't 'ee get too excited, their job has just begun!" So we settled round the table, nudging one another, grinning, ploughing into our delicious breakfast. Breakfast had never tasted so good.

The faithful wireless was switched on. Winston Churchill spoke. "Events in France are a colossal disaster. The whole root and core and brain of the British Army has been stranded at Dunkirk and seems about to perish or be captured."

The mood became sober again but Ma soon rallied us round, telling us to just trust. Something good would happen soon. She was sure of it.

We heard letters fall behind the kitchen door. Lucky, temporarily disturbed from her position behind, carried a letter through to us. And there was another. One addressed to me and the other to Vera.

I quickly tore open the envelope.

'We are pleased to inform Polly Hewitt that she has been successful in gaining a place at Newquay High School. Due to the present position, however, we can only say the place will be held until such time as it can be arranged for her to continue her studies. In the meantime a place will be retained at Padstow School.'

I truly didn't know whether to laugh or cry. My first thought was for Vera, carefully holding her letter.

"You passed, 'av ya Pol?" Vera asked meekly.

"Yes Vera, I have, but what about you?"

"Will you open it for me, Pol - please?"

"We are pleased to inform Vera Emmett, etc., etc..."

"I did it, Pol - I did it, I did it!" Vera's voice rang out and the two of us charged into the garden to tell Ma.

"Well I never - well done, mi darlins - now how are we going to celebrate that news? You must write home girls, straight away, and I'll give you that telephone number, Vera. Your Mam and Dad are going to be so proud of you, Vera, and you too, Polly. What lovely news for your Auntie Jean."

All I could think of was how proud my Mam and Dad would have been.

"Something bothering you, Vera?" I asked my friend.

"What about mi uniform, Pol - Mam and Dad can't afford to buy me uniforms."

Ma overheard this and said "Don't worry darling - there are always uniforms that the girls have outgrown. You might have to do something about that curly mop of yours." Ma crossed the kitchen smiling and ruffled 'the mop'.

"Let's go to Gull House and tell Bernard the news, Vera. I don't think he has a wireless up there".

But we were wrong - Bernard's wireless was perched on his knees whilst he ate his sandwiches. "Hello mi 'andsomes - good news at last and let's hope Denzil, Jimmy and the rest will be back soon. There's a big push to get Gull House ready for casualties. The Boss was running hither and thither this morning like a headless chicken." Indeed the sound of a bulldozer and other machinery invaded the normally tranquil cliff top with noise.

"Like the rabbit - your pup?"

"He loved it Bernard, and so did we, didn't we, Vera?"

"Yes, er - lovely, Bernard" said Vera, but as she turned away she was pinching her nose in disgust.

Dear Aunt Jean,

You will be very happy to hear that both Vera and I did well in the exams and we will BOTH be going to Newquay High School. But not just yet. We have to wait until we are notified by the school.

This is a short letter, Auntie, because we need to help Ma Trewithen.

Love to you and Trouble.

Polly

Dear Mum and Dad

You'll never guess. I passed my exams after all. Polly did too, so I don't have to worry about starting a new school without her. And you don't have to worry about school uniform. The school keeps clothes the older pupils have grown too big for.

Love Vera

Chapter Nine

"Turn on the wireless, Polly, let's hear the news." said Ma. Mr Churchill was speaking again.

He said that the hard and heavy tidings will now be described as a 'miracle' and the British press would announce the evacuation as a disaster turned to triumph. Ma didn't make any attempt at staunching the tears now coursing down her cheeks. He then went on to say "We shall fight them on the beaches", and hailed the rescue as "a miracle of deliverance", and included the miracles of the little ships and the massive part they had played. He declared that St George's Cross defaced with the Arms of Dunkirk would be flown from the jack staff of each and every civilian ship and boat of all sizes that had taken part in the Dunkirk rescue operation.

"But when is Denzil coming home, Ma?" said Billy, standing close to her at the table.

"Might be few days yet, Billy." Ma removed herself and went to get eggs off the nest.

"Denzil's a hero, Vera," I whispered reverently.

"But he's not here yet, Pol - look at Lucky keeping watch. She wants him home, she's not bothered if he's a hero."

Some sixth sense made Ma prepare for Denzil's arrival home. Vera and I went to Bernard for another rabbit. Instead he produced a fine hare.

"Jugged hare, girls, with a nice bunch of vegetables and herbs," Bernard said, proudly holding the naked hare aloft.

Whilst we were talking to Bernard there was a massive rumbling and, coming up the cliff, there were huge lorries carrying beds.

"Stacking up the beds, girls, for the poor lads, I expect. I'll need to go and help them. Enjoy the jugged hare!"

I wished I had been able to tell Auntie about Gull House being prepared for injured men and the house being turned into a hospital, but I thought I should wait until Denzil came home and gave me permission.

By the time the sun had lowered silently over the horizon there was jugged hare bubbling on the range and what looked like the biggest bread and butter pudding in the whole of Cornwall.

"Apples instead of dried fruit, mi darlings - dried fruit's hard to come by."

"It all looks and smells delicious, Ma - is this all for Denzil - do you think he will be home soon?" I asked.

"Pol, I have no idea darling, but the hare can bubble away for a week and, of course, you must have some pudding."

There was plenty of stew to go round and it tasted surprisingly good. The thick, dark gravy, spiced with something tasty, was mopped up with Ma's thick bread and we each had a square of delicious pudding.

Sitting back at the table, 'full to the gunnels' as Denzil would say, we were silent. Lucky had had some hare and then immediately resumed her sentry duties. As the sky darkened we talked of bed, and school as usual tomorrow. But then there was a rumpus behind the kitchen door. Lucky was yapping frantically, scratching with her tiny paws.

"Let her out Vera," said Ma "before she breaks the kitchen door."

Vera opened the kitchen door and Lucky ran out into the dark, leaping straight into Denzil's arms.

Vera, Ma, Billy and Jack stood beside me in silent shock until Ma ran forward and disappeared into Denzil's massive bulk. And then it was chaos and laughter as we all crowded around Denzil at the same time, drawing him into the cottage.

"Something smells good, Ma!" Denzil said, still holding Ma close.

"Billy, Jack, take the tin bath up to my bedroom and fill it with hot water." Ma said.

"Denzil, sit down darlin', eat and then it's off to bed, big man!"

"But Ma! I have to check with the coastguard station and I need to check the lobster pots – and ..."

"Enough, Denzil!" Ma said, firmly in charge.

"Ned's been looking after the lobster pots and the coastguard station can wait."

Denzil only got halfway through the stew and before he was guided to his and Ma's bedroom.

We could hear the oohs and aahs as Denzil lowered himself into the water, and then silence.

We sat in the kitchen, waiting patiently.

"He's home, Polly - Denzil's home!" said Vera quietly.

Ma crept downstairs.

"Time for you to go to bed now, girls! Enough excitement for one evening. Denzil's already asleep."

"Can we just have a peep, Ma, through the door?" I asked.

"Of course, but don't make a noise, Polly."

The four of us climbed the creaking stairs to Ma's bedroom - the door slightly ajar. Denzil was lying on his back already snoring with Lucky high on his shoulder, her cute face under Denzil's beard. Denzil, or Ma, had removed Denzil's eye patch. There was just a slight hollow, nothing more, but he didn't look the same without it. Lucky turned and looked us in the eye as much as to say "He's home - he's mine - now go away and let him sleep." And Denzil did for almost two days.

And whilst he slept, after school, Billy and Jack swabbed, scrubbed and polished Morwenna until she shone once more in the brilliant Padstow light, with no sign of her ordeal.

Strolling with Brian along the quay, we spoke of the previous week with all its anxieties. Padstow lifeboat, along with Jimmy and Brian's Dad, arrived home later than Denzil, along with a few more stragglers. Like Denzil, Jimmy had not yet talked of their ordeals and none of us asked. It was enough to know they were safe, but we knew not everyone involved in "Operation Dynamo" had survived.

To our amazement however, Denzil told us that he had discovered a stowaway after he had left port. He was a French lad, very young and badly injured. Diverting to Mevagissey, Denzil left him in the care of the Red Cross. He said he would tell us more later. We could barely contain our curiosity, but Ma said we should wait until Denzil was ready to tell us more. Anyway, he was very busy now sorting out all the things he had left undone whilst away, including tending to Morwenna which sat, sparkling on the beach after the boys had worked on her.

"You did well, boys!" Denzil beamed.

"An' there I was, sleeping. Thank you."

Billy and Jack hugged Denzil shyly.

"We said we would help if we could, Denzil."

Chapter Ten

As we had missed the May Day celebrations, Ma suggested we have a trip to Rock.

"Ned will give us a lift in his boat as he will be checking his lobster pots, and he can bring us back, too. Lucky can stay with Denzil."

In fact, Lucky hadn't left Denzil's side since his return.

The coastline was vivid with wild orchids, yellow broom, skylarks and bees giddy with clover as they dipped in and out of purple foxgloves. Cornwall looked heavenly. How I wished Aunt Jean could enjoy Cornwall too.

Carrying an enormous picnic basket we boarded Ned's boat. Once again the war seemed very far away.

Ned chatted as we sailed to Rock.

"Any Cornish tales to tell the children, Ned?" asked Ma.

"Well, there is one, Ma."

We sat forward in the boat giving Ned our full attention. Vera felt a bit queasy, so a tale would take her mind off her rumbling tummy.

"It was all the fault of the Siren – a singing mermaid." Ned began.

"Oh, I know all about Sirens, Ned", said Vera importantly.

"Do ee indeed." Ned smiled.

"Padstow would have been a very important port had it not been for the Doombar".

"What's a Doombar?" piped up Jack.

"It's a sand bar Jack. And this particular sand bar was caused by a mermaid who had been singing on the rocks at the entrance to the harbour. People heard her often. Anyway, one day a young hooligan shot at her with his crossbow and in revenge she threw a handful of sand towards the town, forming the fatal Doombar which, ever since, has been a serious threat to shipping. Many gallant ships went across and were lost even."

"Have you ever seen a mermaid, Ned?" Vera asked.

"No midear, but I have heard them singing, especially around Sirens Cave below Gull House.

Ma winked at Ned and Vera winked at me.

"Well, 'eer we are, everyone – have a lovely picnic and I'll pick you up at five p.m. sharp. Give my love to Morwenna, Ma", and off went Ned to do some more fishing.

"What did he mean, Ma?" I asked, "about giving our love to Morwenna?"

But Ma was busy picking red campion and white hyacinth along with some broom.

Jack and Billy carried the picnic basket, with the odd grumble.

"Are we nearly there, Ma?" they both asked.

"Almost, darlin's – just around the point".

And there we were, poised on the high ground, above the beach now with dunes below us, and in the distance Rock village.

"This will be fine; you can put the basket down, boys."

A few feet away we saw a small cairn – a circle of rocks right on the edge of the cliff and, as we approached, we saw it was guarding a tiny headstone. Morwenna's headstone, Ma and Denzil's little girl.

We left Ma to put her flowers at the foot of the stone, watching silently at the peaceful scene. Ma seemed quite relaxed. "Right – tuck in, everyone!" she said cheerily.

We enjoyed our picnic and seeing Ma smile. And, in no time at all, the sun started to dip and five o'clock saw Ned mooring his boat below, and we waved goodbye to Rock and Morwenna until another day.

Chapter Eleven

A few days later, after supper, we were to learn from Denzil about the 'Miracle of the little ships'. The tale had taken on legend status already in Cornwall.

"I'm glad I was able to help," began Denzil modestly.

We all sat around the stove, the boys sticking close to Denzil and taking in every word, Lucky on Denzil's lap.

"Trip down went well, but I lost sight of Jimmy and the life boat. When we got there – to Ramsgate, it was all a rush. The idea was that the small craft could get to the beaches, lift the men and transfer them to the big ships. I lost count of the men and the times we went to and fro. It was the noise, the cries which were worse. Morwenna did well – she was filled to the gunnels each time."

I looked across at Vera. No sniffs, silent for a change. I sidled across and put an arm around her skinny waist. I knew she was thinking about Lionel.

"The beach was being strafed by German aircraft all the time but they were hampered by the weather – thank goodness! The RAF had dogfights (with the Luftwaffe, Billy) covering the retreating troops, but they were losing planes."

"Do you think you've told us enough, Denzil?" asked Ma.

"It's alright, Ma – I'm ready to talk now.

Anyway, the troop ships took everyone to holding camps – the injured to Plymouth.

I dropped off the last of my troops at Ramsgate, including the French. I had the rigging, outboard motor checked at the shipyard, filled her up with water bottles, bread and cheese and blankets – God bless the Red Cross – and set sail for Padstow.

"After dark that first night I moored Morwenna to get some sleep but I heard noises below."

"The Frenchy?" Ma asked.

"The Frenchy." Denzil replied.

"Poor lad. He'd stowed away on Morwenna at Ramsgate and kept quiet below. He kept grabbing my hand and saying "Merci, merci."

"Was he asking for mercy because he thought you were going to kill him, Denzil?" asked wide-eyed Jack.

"No, son – he was saying 'thank you' in French.

He had a really serious leg injury. I poured neat brandy on the leg and into his mouth, poor soul, dressed the leg and then he slept. I couldn't go back to Ramsgate so I decided on dropping him off with the Red Cross in Plymouth. And I did just that.

The reason I'm telling you all this, Ma, is because I want to try and find the lad. I felt bad leaving him."

Ma wasn't surprised and neither were we. And so we sat quietly whilst Denzil and Ma made plans for Denzil to return to try and find the French boy. But he wouldn't be taking Morwenna. He would travel across country.

"It was the fear in his eyes, Ma" said Denzil softly. "He was just a lad!

I can stay with cousin Ben in Saltash for a day or two – if you can manage, Ma. I'll contact the Red Cross to make sure the lad hadn't been taken elsewhere."

"Of course, Denzil." said Ma.

"We'll be fine – won't we, darlin's?"

"We'll take care of Ma, Denzil," Said Billy, sidling up to Denzil.

"I'll take Lucky with me, Ma – she'll get on a treat with Ben's Sally. "Sally is a cross sheepdog, boys. She'll probably think Lucky is one of her lambs."

And we saw Denzil smile for the first time since his return home.

Chapter Twelve

Denzil told us he was hitching a lift with a friend's truck to Plymouth – offering to give him some coupons for petrol. The precious, rationed petrol. He was leaving the following day. Ma packed the usual vegetable pasties and some minced cooked meat and biscuits for Lucky.

Denzil left early, before school, and so we were able to wave him off. As he waved goodbye, Lucky's head appeared at the open window, tongue lolling excitedly.

After they left and just before we set off to school, there was a loud knock at the door. It was George the postboy thrusting something into Ma's hands.

It was a postal telegram addressed to Vera Emmett.

Vera's face turned white as Ma carefully opened the telegram for her, and then handed it to Vera to read.

"Please read it, Ma." Vera pleaded.

"It's addressed to you, midear – you must read it!"

Vera's hands shook.

"It's just four words." She said looking up into Ma's face.

"Well darling?"

"It says, 'Lionel safe. Sends love'."

There was a brief pause and then screams of joy and relief, and dancing around the kitchen table.

Vera said she couldn't wait to get to school to tell Brian. We were all so happy for her, the rest of the morning disappeared into a haze of excitement, relief and joy.

"Vera, darling – you still have porridge round your mouth – go and clean your teeth," said Ma, tracing a finger across Vera's grinning mouth.

"And do something with that hair!"

"I've never seen a telegram before, Vera, can I have a look?" said Billy.

"Ma will show you, Billy!" shouted Vera as she and I rushed around, grabbing school bags.

"Billy – you can see Vera's telegram at tea – off you scoot now, all of you. I have chores to do."

I looked back at Ma waving us off to school. She lifted a hand to her cheek where Vera had plonked a kiss and she was smiling.

"Are you going to write to Lionel tonight, Vera?"

"Oh yes, Ma!" A waft of cabbage drifted towards us as we ran through the school gates. Vera couldn't care less though, in fact she hadn't a care in the world just now.

Chapter Thirteen

We wrote our letters home. Vera and I and posted them immediately. Strolling to the post office, we met Ned working his nets.

"Wonderful news, Vera – he's a lucky boy. Injured is 'ee?"

"I don't know, Ned. I've written a letter, and I'm hoping for one from Lionel soon."

"'Ee's safe, girl – that's the main thing." And Ned returned to his nets.

Vera didn't have long to wait for her precious letter. She had shuffled a lot of the nights following her news and was beginning to look quite pale.

We all sat around her watching trembling hands open the envelope.

"You can read it in our bedroom, Vera".

"No, Polly – I want you all to know about Lionel."

The letter was headed Leeds.

'Dear Vera,

'I am writing this letter in a hospital bed so my writing will be a bit wobbly. Mam and Dad have just left. Mam couldn't stop crying and Dad wasn't much better but it was good to see them.

'They told me what a smashing time you are having in Cornwall and how pleased they are that you are in a safe place. Me too, our kid. They also told me about your war effort and the U-boat. Fancy being in the newspapers. I'm really proud of you, love.

'Denzil is a hero. I hope you all realise that. The sight of all those ships, big and little, coming to rescue us was a wonder.

'I was lucky – many weren't – but I will remember all my life the miracle of those little ships. I hope to meet Denzil one day and thank him myself.

'There is so much to tell, Vera, about the retreat, but I will tell you one wonderful thing.

'As we retreated through France we were followed by a huge pack of dogs. Dogs follow armies because they know they can get food. The dogs had been abandoned. Anyway they followed us all the way to Dunkirk. As we waded through the water towards the little ships they all swam alongside us.

'The ones that survived were handed onto the carriers with us and came to Dover. Not just our pack, but hundreds of them. They will have gone into quarantine because of a terrible disease called rabies. But when they come out they will go to British families. The funny thing is, Vera, they only understand French commands!

'I lost an arm, Vera, in the fighting and so I won't be going back with the lads. Mam and Dad are relieved but I'm worried I'm letting them down.

'I miss you, scallywag! Are you managing to get a brush through that mop of hair?

'Write again soon, lass.

'Love – your brother Lionel. xx'

Chapter Fourteen

"What's 'ee goin' to do for a living, Pol?"

I put an arm around Vera. She had looked sad since receiving Lionel's letter. All the excitement and joy of the postal telegram had gone. The precious telegram was safely locked into Vera's knicker drawer and was taken out each bedtime and read and re-read.

"The important thing is that your brother survived Dunkirk, Vera, and I'm sure he will find something to work at. After all he still has his working hand and arm, otherwise there would have been no letter!"

It was Saturday, the sun was shining and the quay buzzed with the usual mix of mums, babies, toddlers and fisherfolk. And the ever present screeching gulls, of course.

"Let's go for a walk, Vera. It will cheer you up and we can ask Ma if we can go up to see Bernard at Gull House. We can do our clothes later. The boys will be helping Ned with his nets so we can go by ourselves." Vera turned and grinned.

"You're such a pal, Polly. Let's ask Ma if she wants one of Bernard's smelly rabbits. She's missing Denzil and making a rabbit stew will take her mind off him. I wonder when Denzil will be back from Plymouth."

We found Bernard, working hard in what remained of his garden.

"Well I never – you come to see old Bernard or is it another of my rabbits you're after?"

"A rabbit would be lovely." I said.

We followed him to his shed and he took down one of the rabbits, wrapping it in old newspaper.

"I 'eerd about your brother, Vera – how's 'ee doin'?"

"He's just written." said Vera softly.

"Bad news was it?"

"He's lost an arm but he can still write, so maybe he will be able to work." Vera struggled to smile.

"Goodness me, yes Vera. He won't be going back – so that will please your Mam and Dad. How old is he?"

"Lionel's eighteen."

"Just a lad – 'e'ell soon bear up and you must do the same. Wait until you see the lads when they arrive here at Gull House – there'll be all sorts!"

"When will they arrive, Bernard?" I asked.

"Any time now, Polly, any time. They're almost ready for them up at the House. Nurses in sparkling white uniforms rushing hither and thither and all the beds in their places. It's good to see the old house being used for some good after all that went on there."

"Thanks for the rabbit. 'Bye, Bernard."

The old bag containing the rabbit swung between us as we climbed down to the quay and the cottage.

"Do you think we can help up at the house, Poll – I mean when we are not at school?"

"What a brilliant idea, Vera! I would love that and I wouldn't mind what jobs we were asked to do. I'm quite excited, let's see what Ma thinks."

Already Vera had cheered up.

"I think that's a splendid idea, girls. I will go up to the House when I have a minute and speak to someone in charge. I don't suppose they will want you in the way, but they might be grateful for the offer."

Ma was busy skinning the rabbit so Vera and I left the kitchen.

"I hate it when she has to do that – skin the rabbit, I mean. All in one go, like taking its overcoat off".

"But you enjoy the stew, Vera, don't you?"

"Oh yes, when it's served up in little chunks with veg and gravy and some of Ma's dumplings. I'm hungry already." And Vera grinned like her usual self.

Chapter Fifteen

The old wireless was on after we got back from school. Something about the Battle of the Atlantic.

"What does it all mean, Ma?" Billy asked Ma whilst they fed the hens.

"Convoys of ships carrying food to us, Billy, being attacked by those blessed U-boats. Trying to starve us out, I suppose. Don't you worry your head, Billy – Bernard's got plenty of rabbits and Denzil will catch the fish, and don't forget our hens. Which reminds me, there's a hole in the fence around the hen coop – do you think you and Jack could mend that for me after your school work?"

Ma barely had time to turn around before Billy grabbed the hammer from Denzil's box of tools and ran off, followed eagerly by Jack.

"Those lads 'ave been good since Denzil left. 'Bout time he was home though," said Ma, gazing through the window to the quay.

Vera and I agreed. We missed Denzil and Lucky.

"Bless me, I know what that racket is!"

Ma opened the kitchen door and in flew Lucky, not knowing who to greet first, but with a nose in the air smelling rabbit stew followed closely by Denzil.

The boys ran in from the hen coop and all of us threw arms around Denzil, Ma looking over the tops of our heads, arms folded, grinning from ear to ear.

"'Ello my 'andsome. Welcome home!"

Rabbit stew with dumplings never tasted so good. We, all of us, sat around the kitchen table with Denzil at the head, tucking into the delicious meal.

Lucky had her share then sank down beside Denzil's chair.

"I expect you will want to know all about my trip before you go to bed."

"I had a lift all the way to Plymouth and Lucky and I were spoiled by cousin Ben. Lucky was shadowed by Ben's dog, Sally. I was very proud of Lucky. She's been a good pup." Denzil leant down and stroked the silky head.

"What about the boy, Denzil?" Ma asked anxiously.

"Well – I found 'im thanks to the Red Cross. He's still in hospital but will be moved shortly. They couldn't save his leg though. The hospital was full to the gunnels with injured."

I looked across to Vera who was listening intently to Denzil but she didn't interrupt.

"He will have to stay in Plymouth a while longer, but then I suggested that maybe he could come here to, Padstow to convalesce. I'm not sure yet whether his doctor would approve, but I said I felt it might be helpful, him knowing me. Anyway we will have to wait and see."

"What's he called, Denzil?" asked Vera.

"His name is Henri – Henry to us. His mother was Irish but she's passed on and, of course, his father's French. He's not sure where his father is right now. His English is good. Anyway, enough of me. Any more stew, Ma?"

"Go on, Vera, tell Denzil your news," Ma urged Vera, squeezing her hand.

"Mi brother's safe Denzil – I got a postal telegram from Mam and Dad!"

"Well – that's wonderful news, darling!" said Denzil, raising himself from his chair and hugging Vera.

"Something amiss, Vera?" Denzil asked gently.

"Well, he, he lost an arm, Denzil, but he can still write" Vera quickly added.

"No more injuries then?"

"He hasn't said so. I think he's just pleased to be home. Well, he is in hospital still in Leeds at Potternewton, where they take care of war injured. Mam and Dad try and see him every day – I wish I could."

And Vera covered her face with her hands, her body shaking.

Lucky was quickly by Vera's side, nudging her.

"Oh, my love," Ma said, putting an arm around Vera.

"Let those tears flow and you will feel better. You've been a brave girl – hasn't she, Polly?"

"Vera's the bravest girl I have ever met." I replied.

Chapter Sixteen

School seemed very boring over the next few days following all the events of the past week, except for Brian, of course, who was eager to ask lots of questions. Billy and Jack were showing off, answering questions about Denzil's return to Plymouth to find Henri.

"Henri's French, you know, Mavis." Jack was overheard talking to a friend in class.

"Denzil saved his life!" Billy interrupted.

"Will Denzil get a medal?" asked a wide-eyed Mavis.

"Oh, I expect so!" Billy pushed out his chest importantly.

"Maybe a gold one!"

"Ooo," was all Mavis could manage to say.

"Settle down children please, and take out your arithmetic notebooks. Mavis, return to your seat!"

"What did you tell everyone, Billy?" I asked him at play break.

"No fibs – honestly, Polly!" said Billy.

"Good – we don't want everyone in Padstow to know our business, Billy. Denzil trusts us not to chatter." I hugged Billy so he would know I wasn't cross.

"Well – you know what they say, Billy." Vera joined in.

"Walls have ears."

"That's a bit daft, Vera!" said Billy.

"It means, during wartime, we are not supposed to talk too much. We might accidentally give away a secret."

"That's enough, you two – back to class," and I pushed Billy gently through the door to his class.

There wasn't much 'chat'. People in Padstow had their own problems, and there was always so much work to do. Only Ned, as we passed him on the quay, waved hello.

Later, taking the hens' eggs from the coop, I was startled by an unusual sound. At first I thought it was a tractor in the top field but it got louder. As I turned away from the hens' nest I saw an aircraft approaching the hill behind Quay Cottage. We were used to seeing aircraft approaching us on their return from patrolling the seas and on their way back to the airfield at St Eval. But this plane was very low with a plume of smoke trailing behind. It disappeared over the hill, but then there was a loud crunching thump. I dropped the bucket of eggs and ran inside, calling for Ma.

"I heard it, Polly darling. Look, there's Ned running to Denzil," said Ma, looking through the kitchen window. Ma was very calm.

Denzil rushed up from the beach.

"Where's Vera, Ma?" Denzil asked.

"I'm here, Denzil! I was just tidying my room. What was that big noise just now?"

"Looks like an aircraft has crash landed over the top field. The coastguard will be alerting the police and ambulance, and the airfield at St Eval. Best you all stay put and out of the way. I'll get back as soon as I can."

Of course Lucky wanted to go with Denzil but we had to keep her in the kitchen with us. She was scratching frantically at the door and refused to be cuddled. But she changed her mind when Ma gave her a bit of cold rabbit.

"I <u>knew</u> something bad was going to happen!" Vera whispered to me.

"Whatever do you mean, Vera?"

"I could hear the Siren," Vera said, close to my ear.

"Oh Vera – don't be silly."

"I 'eard her when we were coming back with the rabbit from Gull House. It was faint and I know you didn't hear anything, but I did, Poll!"

Chapter Seventeen

Denzil returned to the cottage with the news that 'one of our lads', as he put it, had indeed crash-landed in the top field. He was heading for the church at St Eval close to the airfield after patrolling the Atlantic, and the church with its high tower was clearly visible to aircrew making their way home.

"Anyway," Denzil said, "the pilot was unhurt and able to scramble free before his aircraft exploded."

We frequently heard and saw aircraft flying overhead on the return to St Eval, but it hadn't occurred to us children how dangerous their missions were.

It was the following day that I overheard Vera telling me she had heard the Siren again. Or thought she had. Since Vera's fall down the disused mineshaft that dark night of the dramatic events at Gull House, she hadn't spoken of the Siren. Denzil had said the singing she thought she had heard was just the underground water below the disused mineshaft. She had never been convinced. Even Ned mentioning the Siren had prompted her to make a comment. Now, I wanted to know what she meant when she said she had heard the Siren again.

"It was when we were walking back with the rabbit. We were close to the edge of the cliff on the path and you had just gone ahead of me. I heard her, I'm sure I did, Polly."

"OK Vera, let's retrace our steps this evening after chores and you can show me." I grasped Vera's hand. "You know I do listen, Vera."

It was a beautiful evening when we set off for the cliff walk, the drama of the crashed aircraft behind us. All we could hear, above the sound of the approaching tide, were the seagulls, swooping overhead and over Gull House.

Lucky ran ahead, Denzil's spotted handkerchief around her neck, her ears flapping in the breeze. She was having fun but then she disappeared from sight.

"Oh no!" Vera called her.

"Lucky, Lucky come back, you naughty pup!"

No Lucky.

"I knew we should have kept her on her string," said Vera anxiously.

"Don't worry, Vera, she knows where we are. She'll come back." I tried to convince myself.

And just when we were really beginning to panic – there was her high, insistent bark coming from below us.

We stepped carefully forward and looked over the edge of the cliff.

Lucky was below, on the beach, tearing backwards and forwards around a dark shape between the rocks.

"She's found something, Polly – look, she's telling us she's found something." Vera clutched at my sleeve.

"Can you hear her, Pol – the Siren – it's the sound I heard – it's coming from below!" Vera's eyes shone with excitement.

"We have to get down to Lucky, Polly!"

"Vera, let's walk a little further and get down to the beach on Ruthen Steps – the steps close to Siren's Cave, it will be safer!"

We hurried a little further up the path, keeping a lookout for Lucky. She was now lying down on the sand watching 'the shape'.

The steps were slippery but soon we were on the beach walking carefully towards Lucky.

"Well I never," said Vera softly.

"What, Vera, what?" I tried to catch up with her.

"It's an animal and it's caught between the rocks, Polly."

As I approached I saw Lucky had found a beautiful grey seal.

"It's a seal, Vera – I've seen lots on holidays on the coast with Aunty. I think it's a grey seal!"

Then we heard the cry – it came from inside Siren's Cave. We hadn't been into Siren's Cave for a long time. The cave that sat beneath the cliff top house – Gull House.

"Oh – it's the Siren, Pol – it's her," whispered Vera close to me.

"No, Vera – I think it's a seal pup, and this is her mother." We looked down on the creature gazing up with soulful eyes at us.

All this time Lucky stayed very still and quiet as if she knew that the seal was in trouble.

"Let's have a look for the pup, Vera. The tide will be in very soon!" I grabbed her hand as we went into the cave. We didn't have to walk very far inside before we found the pup, bigger than I had anticipated. It was caught around its neck with what looked like netting.

"Now – we have to get help – quickly, Vera!"

"You can run faster than me. Take Lucky with you and run up to Gull House and find Bernard – he'll know what to do. I will stay here. Please hurry, Vera, you know how quickly the tide turns."

Vera didn't waste a moment — quickly putting the string on Lucky's spotted kerchief the pair raced back to Ruthen Steps.

I watched them climb to the top and turned to watch the grey seal, its huge eyes locked on mine. "Windows to the soul," seals' eyes, Polly" I remembered Aunty's words.

I sat with the grey seal, not daring to go too close. The pup's cries inside Siren's Cave echoed against the vastness inside.

The mother turned away from my gaze. Then a boat came around the point, two aboard waving to me on the beach.

It was Denzil of course, dear Denzil, with Brian's dad, Jimmy.

They stopped the outboard motor as they drew closer, finally jumping off and drawing the boat up on the beach.

"Now my handsome, what have you found?"

Denzil spoke gently, drawing closer to the grey seal.

"Oh Denzil, thank you for coming, and you Jimmy!"

"There's a pup in Siren's Cave, Denzil, can you hear it?"

"I can, Polly. Come on Jimmy, let's go and see what we can do but first we must see how the mother is."

Jimmy and Denzil examined the seal from a distance but it was clear she had become wedged between two rocks, injuring herself in an attempt to release her bulky body. There was a wound in her side which must have happened on the tide's turn.

I stayed with the seal, talking softly to her.

"It's alright – Denzil will look after you, you poor thing."

But what would Denzil and Jimmy do?

Denzil and Jimmy went back to the boat and took out what looked like two large sheets of tarpaulin.

"The pup's ok – no more than a month old, I'd say, but we have to release the net around her neck."

"I'd say the same, Denzil," said Jimmy.

"Let's get the pup first, Jim, and put it in the boat, then come back for the mother."

"Where are you going to take them, Denzil?"

"We'll take them to the wonderful lady at St Agnes who has a way with the creatures. She has a big pool by the house and cares for injured seals until they are ready for release. We'll sail round the point and do the rest by road in Jimmy's truck. Let's hope they both survive the journey. One thing is sure. The pair must leave soon before the next high tide. Will you be able to get home on your own, Polly?"

"I'm on my way, Denzil, as soon as I see you and Jimmy on board!"

Denzil and Jimmy – big and strong as they are – had no difficulty getting mother and pup into the boat, the pup making noises as it came close to its mother. Both were wrapped into the tarpaulin after Denzil had doused them with sea water.

"Vera, you ran so fast up Ruthen Steps, I thought you had sprouted wings!" I said later.

"Tell Polly – please tell – tell!" said Billy and Jack excitedly.

And so there was yet another tale to tell about Siren's Cave.

Chapter Eighteen

It was Friday – everyone in school loved Friday. The whole weekend stretched before us. We could have free time to do whatever we wanted. Billy and Jack would want to help Denzil with Morwenna. She would be swabbed down, her rigging checked and inside the cabin would be dusted, washed and polished. The boys loved Denzil's boat. No one would ever guess they were Leeds city boys who had never even seen the sea before their evacuation.

"Now girls – come here and listen." Vera and I sat at the kitchen table with Ma.

"This might be the time to go up to the hospital at Gull House and see what they think about you two volunteering some of your time. What do you think?"

"When Ma?" Vera asked.

"Too late this evening – we'll walk up tomorrow, girls!"

We both found it hard to get to sleep that night, thinking about going up to Gull House with Ma. We were excited but wondered what we would be able to do to help

"I hope there's not too much screaming and – and blood to see!" Vera emphasized the blood.

"Well, there must be some, Vera, although Gull House is a sort of resting place for the men that have been injured. It will be fine. Anyway, the matron and doctors may not want us there. Let's wait and see!"

Ma told us to make sure we were wearing clean dresses and socks. "Hospital places have to be kept very clean and tidy, girls," Ma emphasized.

I plaited Vera's unruly mop, she tidied my hair and we left straight after breakfast. The boys waved to us from the quay where Morwenna was tied up. I think Jack shouted something rude, but he was smiling. We saw Denzil give him a playful clip around the ear.

It was very busy at Gull House. There were lots of nurses in crisp blue and white uniforms with red crosses on the front of their aprons and two doctors passed us as we came through the front door, in pristine white coats.

"Can I help you?" One of the nurses stopped us.

"Please can we have a word with Matron?" Ma asked.

"Do you have an appointment?"

"No – but it won't take a minute," said Ma.

"What's that horrible smell?" Vera whispered in my ear.

"Antiseptic, Vera – have you never been to a hospital before?"

"No – the doctor took my tonsils out on our kitchen table, Mam said."

"Vera," said Ma. "if you want to help here you will have to get used to that smell. It's to keep away infection – you know, germs. Are you sure you want to be here, darling – you don't have to, you know!"

"I think so, Ma."

Vera didn't sound too sure to me.

Matron looked a bit stern but she had a very soft voice.

"It is extremely kind of you to offer to help, girls." Matron spoke to us across a huge table.

"If you want to help I'm sure there will be lots of things that you can do. The nurses are, of course, extremely busy as you have probably noticed. And we are expecting more patients next week. How about coming again tomorrow – Sunday – and we will arrange something for you both. Will you be with them, Mrs Trewithen?"

" Er – no, Matron. There are two more evacuees to look after at home, and my husband!"

"Of course." Matron said, raising herself from behind her desk and showing us to the door.

"Well – Polly and Vera – we will see you tomorrow morning."

"What a nice lady, girls. I'm sure you will be fine. What do you think, Vera?"

"Well – er ,yes Ma. I'll be all right with Polly."

"That's my girls." Ma hugged us both.

"How about fish and chips for tea as a treat?"

Chapter Nineteen

"I've got some news, everyone!" said Denzil as he came through the kitchen door.

Young Henri is coming to Gull House from Plymouth along with three more injured next week. I'll give him a day or two to settle in, and then contact Matron to see if I can visit!"

"We have news too, Denzil," I said.

"Matron said we can help at Gull House. She wants to see us tomorrow afternoon after Chapel."

"Are you both going then?" Denzil asked, starting on his bowl of soup.

"Well I will, Denzil, but I'm not sure about Vera!"

"Where's the lass now?"

"She's taken some eggs next door, Denzil." said Ma, her hands on her ever present apron.

"She's a bit sensitive to smells, is our Vera," Ma smiled.

"She will get used to them, I'm sure," I said to Ma, joining Denzil at the table.

Just then Vera walked in.

"Vera, come and sit down midear, after you've washed your hands."

"What's up?" Vera dried her hands and joined us at the table.

"Just wondering if you really want to come up to Gull House with me, Vera."

"It's the smell Pol, and – Gull House – all those memories of that 'orrible housekeeper!"

"She's gone, Vera." I touched her knee under the table.

"And will never come back. It's alright though, you know, I won't mind going on my own. I really want to help. There's no point in you going if it's going to make you unhappy."

I could almost feel the sense of relief coming from Vera, her shoulders relaxing.

"Settled, girls." Ma wiped her hands yet again on the apron.

"Vera – you can help me, darling – lots to do down here at the cottage. So stop worrying."

Matron didn't seem to mind when I arrived the following afternoon on my own.

"Any help will be appreciated, Polly. Now come with me and I will take you to meet Sister!"

Sister smiled and shook hands and gave me a short list of things I could do to help.

"More injured coming in a few days, Polly — what a sweet name! When we have a break you must tell me all about yourself."

"There's a French boy coming to Gull House, Sister, that Denzil helped to rescue and he told us he would be arriving with the injured soon. Denzil is going to ask you if he can come and see him. His name is Henri!"

"Goodness, you have news well ahead of me." Sister smiled.

"I'm sure the lad will be pleased to see someone he has met before. I'm not sure how badly he is injured though, Polly, and the final word will have to be with Matron, and the doctors of course!"

I was led forward to wards and started on my little list.

Vera would definitely not like the smell of antiseptic, but the beds were set up in an orderly fashion and all the patients seemed to be asleep.

How strange that Gull House's dining room and drawing room now housed all these injured men. It seemed a very long time ago since we were here – held against our will - but in fact it was only a few months ago.

Chapter Twenty

I walked back down the cliff road to Quay Cottage, my head still full of the various tasks Sister had given me to do. She had given me a white coat to wear over my frock which made me feel like a proper nurse.

"You tired, Polly?" Ma asked.

"Not really, Ma – in fact I had a lovely time helping Sister. I prepared bandages – rolled them that is, and cleaned out the sluice room – that's where all the instruments and things are kept, I think, but best of all I talked to some of the patients and even read a bit to one of them. I think I must have washed my hands a hundred times, Ma – look, they're still pink!"

"Sit down, Polly and have some tea – I'm really proud of you darling, but you have school tomorrow, so you must rest up!"

Later I told Vera all about my time at Gull House.

"Honestly Vera, Gull House looks completely different, just like a proper hospital. Lots of beds lined up down the dining room, the same in the drawing room. And everything is sparkly clean."

"Lots of smells though, I expect," said Vera curling up her nose.

"A few – but I did get used to them, as the day went on. What have you been doing today? I missed you!"

"Oh go on, Polly – you never did," said Vera glowing pink.

Curled up in our bed Vera and I talked of the far away war. If it hadn't been for the news on Ma's old wireless and the planes flying over the cottage on their return to the airfield at St Eval, we could be in another world.

Vera had written to Lionel twice since his return home. He seemed to be doing well, she said, his letter always cheerful, "But he always is cheerful, Pol, our Lionel. Dad always calls him chippy cheerful. Dad said the two of them are planning to go for a pint of Guinness to 'The Grapes' public house as soon as Lionel's ready. What a sight that will be. Three legs and three arms between them!"

I looked closely at Vera over the bedclothes to see if she was alright, but she was giggling.

"Vera, I think I know what I want to do when I leave school."

"Don't tell me – a nurse!" Vera turned to look at me.

"Yes."

"You mean you actually like all those smells and blood and sick!"

"Well, yes. At least I don't mind them."

"Ya mad, Pol!" And Vera disappeared under her bedsheet.

"Maybe, but that's how I feel at the moment. Take your cold feet, Vera Emmett, to the other side of the bed!"

The giggling started again.

I knew one thing for sure. I had only known Vera for such a short time but she felt like the sister I never had.

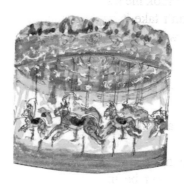

Chapter Twenty-One

"I've got a surprise for you all today." Vera, Billy, Jack and I lifted our eyes from the breakfast table and looked up to Ma who was grinning.

"A picnic, Ma?" Billy asked.

"We going fishin' Ma?" piped up Jack.

"No, we are all off to Summercourt Fair. Denzil has work and he will have Lucky, because we need to catch the one and only bus we have this week. But the hens need to be cleaned out and fed first, beds made and a picnic made. We can catch the bus at 11 o'clock. Now, have any of you ever been to a fair?"

"We had a fair at Woodhouse Moor in Leeds, Ma," piped up Vera.

"You ever been, Pol?" asked Vera.

"Oh yes. Auntie took me last year and I won a goldfish on one of the stalls. I didn't take it home though because of Trouble, our cat. And there were toffee apples, and chips-in-a-bag and even candy floss!"

"What about you boys, have you ever been to a fair?" asked Ma.

"No, we didn't 'ave enough spare money, did we Billy?"

"Right, all the more reason to go, boys. I've raided the egg money. There won't be much to spend but I'm sure we can manage two shillings each!"

"Ma – that's a fortune!" said Vera excitedly.

"Well, you deserve a treat – you surely do," said Ma.

We could hear the noise of the fair as soon as we got off the bus, and there was such a buzz of excitement as we got closer to the field and so many people.

There were stalls with games, swingingboats and even a helter-skelter. I could also smell a warm waft of chips-in-a-bag reminding me of home, Auntie and Trouble. She would be so pleased to hear all about our visit.

"Girls, keep an eye on the boys and I will just sit here and have a rest."

"Of course, Ma. Boys, stay close to Vera and me – don't stray away, please. Come on then, who wants a ride on the swingingboats. We can all get into one."

The sounds, smells and colours were so exciting. I do wish Auntie could be here to share them.

"Don't look so glum, Pol." Vera grabbed my arm and the next minute I was pulled into the swingboat and the ropes were pulling us higher and higher. The boys were screaming with delight and, so far, nobody said they felt sick.

Recovering our land legs we then went over to one of the stalls. Billy hooped a duck and won a sweet-on-a-stick. Jack tried his luck on the rifle range. Vera spotted something else and whispered in my ear.

"Polly, I think that tent belongs to a gipsy, the orange one over there, and she tells fortunes. Shall we go?"

"I think we should ask Ma first, Vera."

"Why, Pol?"

"I just do. You watch the boys and I'll go across and ask. I've only got sixpence left anyway."

Ma looked concerned for a moment before replying.

"I'm not sure, darling. I don't 'old with no fortune-telling."

"But it's only a bit of fun, Ma, I'm sure."

"Oh well, you and Vera can go but not the boys – they're a bit too young, Polly."

The inside of the tent was really dark but there was just enough light to see a strangely, dressed lady at a small table in the middle. On the table was a ball, made of crystal. She sat with her long fingers curled around it. Her fingernails were about two inches long!

"Come in midears and sit down." She held out her hand.

"You must cross my palm with silver."

"Well, here goes your last sixpence, Pol." Vera whispered.

"What about you, my dear?" said the gipsy turning to Vera.

"Oh, I don't 'ave any money left, Missus!"

"Then you must stay very quiet."

"Oh I will, I will." Vera sat down on the grass beside my chair.

"You're young, darlin', but you've had sadness in your life," said the gipsy, "but all will be well, midear – just be patient."

I sat still, hardly daring to breathe.

"You have a strong will and a kind heart and that's a good match. You have a long life line, too."

She turned my palm upwards and stroked my fingers.

"I see a large house on a cliff."

My heart thumped in my chest and Vera grabbed my leg.

"You have had connections with the house. Some bad, very bad, but now I see light and sun and kindness. A lot of kindness. You are part of that kindness, darling. I can see it here, in the crystal." The crystal seemed to glow.

"Well mi 'andsome, I think that's enough for now. Thank you for coming to see an old lady. Better take your friend and go to the kind lady who looks after you."

Walking back to Ma, Vera grabbed my hand.

"'Ow did she know Ma was a kind lady?"

"I've no idea, Vera. She probably just guessed."

Billy and Jack were sitting with Ma, eating their chips-in-a-bag.

"Well then, darlin's, everything all right?"

"She didn't say very much Ma," I said, looking at Vera.

"Did she say you will meet a tall, dark stranger called Brian?" Billy teased.

"Shurrup Billy – Brian's our friend!" said Jack, nudging Billy.

"Now you two – behave. Come on, let's be getting the bus home."

"Mi Mam used to buy clothes pegs and lace handkerchiefs from the gipsies that knocked at our door, Polly," said Billy. "She said if she didn't buy anything, the gipsy would put a curse on her!"

"Stuff and nonsense Billy. Now come along do, or we'll be walking all the way home to Quay Cottage."

Chapter Twenty-Two

Sunday morning started bright and early – except for Vera, that is. She was still tucked into her bedclothes, spikes of hair topping the sheet.

"I'm off then, Vera – are you sure you wouldn't like to come with me to help at Gull House?"

"Mm – no thanks, I'm lovely and cosy. 'Bye Pol."
I really didn't like leaving Vera behind.

"'Bye Ma. I'm off."

"Bye darling, there's a good girl!"

I saw Sister as I approached the house. She looked pristine and busy. I wasn't sure whether I should speak – but then, "Good day, Polly – how nice to see you, dear. Where's your friend?"

"Vera's not sure, Sister, whether she can cope with a few things – smells mainly!"

To my surprise Sister laughed.

"I was exactly the same when I first started nursing, dear. One gets used to all sorts of experiences at the outset. Perhaps Vera would prefer just talking to the patients in our grounds, especially as the weather is so lovely. See what she says, Polly. By the way, our new patients arrive this afternoon so there are beds to be made up!"

I couldn't restrain my excitement, and wished the time away until my chores were finished.

Vera was taking eggs from the hen house when I got back.

"Vera, Vera come and listen. How do you fancy coming along with me next time I go to Gull House? Sister says you can be outside with the patients in the garden. No smells, Vera, and they would be so grateful, the nurses I mean. You might even be able to bring Lucky with you – but I will have to check first."

Vera turned round to face me with a basket full of eggs with a lovely big grin. "You promise, Pol – no smells?"

"I do, Vera, I do! I have missed you, you know, and the patients would love to meet you. You can write letters home for them – or read to them. What do you say, Vera?"

"I'll do it, Pol – if they want me up there. I'll do it!"

We walked back to the cottage hugging one another, and surprised Ma trying to make the best of a suet pudding with raisins for supper.

"What a wonderful idea, Polly. That Sister sounds like a really nice nurse."

Ma whispered to me. "Polly – Vera has missed you – quite lost without her mate, Polly darling."

That same evening the old wireless spluttered out the news that London was being bombed almost nightly. There were many casualties.

"It's terrible, terrible, the poor souls." Ma dabbed her eyes with the corner of her apron.

The boys and Denzil joined us for supper and the news was still the same. Ma turned off the wireless. "Nothing we can do except pray – nothing."

"I'm glad we don't come from London, Polly" said Jack mournfully.

"How far away is London from Leeds, Denzil?"

Denzil looked thoughtful for a few moments.

"A fair distance Jack, and still a long way from here." Denzil looked across at Ma and took her hand across the table.

As if to lighten the atmosphere, Denzil turned to me and said, "By the way - Matron said can you both go up to Gull House and see Henri, but she wants me to go alone first, Polly!"

"We understand Denzil, but please ask Matron if Vera and I can go up on Saturday instead of after Chapel on Sunday."

"Will do, darling."

"I'll make the lad some soda bread, girls, and give you a pat of butter and jam."

"Oo Ma, can we have some too?" Billy said.

"Would I forget my boys?" said Ma hugging Billy.

And Lucky stirred from her slumber to run round and round the table to join in the fun. It felt as if the sun had come out.

Chapter Twenty-Three

"How was Henri, Denzil?"

"Well, everybody – he seems to be doing fine. He's only a young lad, and the wounds are healing well and he can manage to get around the ward with crutches. Plucky lad – that's for sure.

His English is very good but then his mother was Irish. Doesn't seem to know what happened to his Dad. He disappeared just before the Germans invaded France. The mother died some time ago.

"Matron said it is alright for you girls to visit Henri, but don't take Lucky just yet. We don't want her tripping the lad up over his crutches."

Ma's soda bread smelt delicious. Warm wafts floated up the stairs to our bedroom.

"You excited, Polly?" asked Vera over the bedclothes.

"Of course not, Vera – whatever do you mean?"

"Well – 'ee might be 'ansome as a prince, Pol, and it might be love at first sight!" Vera giggled wickedly.

"Don't be silly, Vera – go to sleep!"

But I couldn't sleep. I didn't know any French and had certainly never met a French boy. Would he have dark hair and blue eyes?

Would he want to meet two girls as young as us? Would he even care?

Vera was already snoring gently as I slipped quietly out of our bed, opened the curtains just a few inches and looked over the water to Rock. To the side, above the cliff, stood Gull House – in darkness because of the blackout curtains. I wondered which bed was Henri sleeping in? Was he sleeping? Or was he thinking of home and his missing father?

"Right, girls – off you go with your basket. Vera, you don't have to stay up at Gull House as long as Polly – you can come back when you like, darlin'!"

The basket was loaded with sweet-smelling soda bread and a jar of Ma's jam. I would give it to Sister to share amongst the men, but I would keep one soda bread back just in case Henri missed out.

"Gull House still gives me the shivers, Polly," said Vera walking beside me.

"Oh Vera, you wouldn't recognise it – you'll see how different it all looks soon. Look, there's Bernard!"

"Well, well, if it isn't the maids from Quay Cottage" shouted Bernard, taking off his cap and waving it to us.

Bernard stopped in his tracks, leaning on his barrow whilst we caught up with him.

"You come to do some nursing, girls?"

"Bernard, Sister lets me do all sorts of useful things, but not quite nursing yet," I said.

"But Vera has come along to see if she can chat to the men — keep them company, you know, and later she can bring Lucky to meet them."

Sister was walking towards us from the top path.

"Girls — how lovely to see you both. Come along with me and I will take you both to meet Henri. Mr Trewithen called by earlier and said you were on your way." Sister took the basket and thanked us.

I watched Vera's face closely as we walked through to the ward. I do hope she wasn't sick or faint or anything.

She didn't say a word, but watched Sister closely.

"Now, Polly dear, can you first of all come along with me to get some fresh bed linen from store. Vera, you can come along too and help Vera make up some beds."

We carried the sparklingly clean sheets back to the ward and Sister left us.

"Where are the patients, Polly?" Vera asked.

"Probably outside in the sunshine. Denzil calls them the 'walking wounded,' Vera, which means they don't have to stay in their beds all the time."

"But where's Henri?"

"I don't know, but help me change these two beds and we'll try and find out."

"You were a big help, Vera – with the beds, I mean."

"You're a good teacher Pol, and anyway Mam used to get me to make the beds at home but I've never folded the corners, though. You learn something every day."

And I watched Vera grinning to herself and, in fact, she was humming quietly under her breath.

"Well done girls, now come with me and I will take you to meet Henri. He had a little set back so is confined to bed."

He was terribly pale, the young man lying in the corner bed. He seemed to be sleeping so we approached him quietly. He looked so young and vulnerable like a little boy with the sheet tucked under his chin.

His hair was raven black against his white face.

He had a cage over his lower body to keep the sheets clear of his wounds.

Vera took my hand and whispered. "He looks like our Lionel, Pol – they could be brothers!"

Chapter Twenty-Four

We arrived back from school to a very sad Quay Cottage and a worried-looking Ma and Denzil. The boys had called at Brian's house on their way home and hadn't arrived back yet.

"Is something the matter, Ma?" Vera and I asked anxiously.

"Had a visit from the welfare lady, girls." Ma turned to Denzil.

"Should we tell the girls, Denzil?"

"Yes Ma, it concerns all of us."

Vera went pale.

"The nice lady said she had had a letter from Billy and Jack's mother to say their father had disappeared just before the end of his leave, and she was left to look after his aging mother. She said that she is worried she won't be able to cope looking after her mother-in-law and the boys, should they be returned to her like some of the children who have been sent back home having been evacuated?"

At this point Ma dabbed her eyes with her apron, and Denzil continued.

"I said to the young woman that Billy and Jack can stay with us as long as they want, no matter what the circumstances, and that the authorities must reassure their mother that they are safe and she mustn't worry. Sounds to me she has enough on her hands, poor soul."

"Poor lads," said Vera tearfully.

"Now don't fret, Vera darling, we will all take care of the boys – no matter what – just as Denzil says."

"But his father – where has he gone?" I asked.

Denzil answered "Nobody seems to know, Polly. Gone AWOL for whatever reason. We mustn't judge him – not our place!"

"What's AWOL, Denzil?" Vera asked the inevitable question.

"It means Absent Without Leave, Vera. A very serious offence. Didn't return to duty after his leave. It means a Court-Martial if they catch him. Who knows why he disappeared. Anyway, that has nothing to do with us. The lady from welfare is coming again tomorrow to speak to the boys personally. I'm sure she will find the right words. We must encourage the boys to write to their Ma a bit more.

Vera and I were out when the welfare lady came back to speak to Billy and Jack.

"We've had a special lady come to see us, Polly," said Jack later.

"A very important lady," added Billy.

"What did she say, boys?" I barely dared ask.

"Oh, she just said Mam was looking after Granny and that Dad had gone off somewhere at the end of his leave, and that Mam was having a rum old time looking after Gran. Mam told the lady that she wouldn't be able to cope, looking after all of us, if we were sent back to Leeds yet. The lady asked us if we were happy here, and we both said – very happy Mrs, – didn't we, our Jack?"

"We 'ave to write to Mam though more often, Polly – will you help us?" pleaded Billy.

"Of course, boys – and a few drawings as well, Billy – you're good at drawing."

Chapter Twenty-Five

School seemed boring now, we couldn't wait for the summer holidays to begin. Perhaps Vera and I could spend more time at Gull House. But we had to help Ma with the chores and the boys.

Billy had his ninth birthday last week and Jack would be ten in August. We had already planned a joint birthday celebration for Jack and me. So much seemed to have happened since my eleventh birthday and Vera's too.

The boys had taken their news well and the welfare lady was relieved that Ma and Denzil were happy to keep them here in Padstow.

"Come with me, girls," said Sister.

"Is it alright to have Lucky with us, Sister?"

"Of course, Vera – she's a jolly little dog with her spotted handkerchief collar."

"Henri – here are your new friends. This is Polly and this is Vera and this is Lucky. Girls, this is Henri Bovour."

Lucky went straight to Henri and licked the lowered hand.

"I will leave you to get to know one another, but I need you in a while, Polly dear – shall we say – half an hour?"

"I am very pleased to meet you, Polly and Vera," said Henri holding out his hand.

Vera and I shook it and were shocked into silence. Henri looked so much better out here in the garden. He was still a little pale but his eyes were bright and there was a little colour in his cheeks. How handsome, I thought. There was a rug over his lap. Lucky tried to jump up onto Henri's lap.

"Oh no, Lucky, that's naughty." Vera chastised Lucky.

"No matter, Vera, she isn't heavy – are you, little girl?" And Henri stroked Lucky's silky head.

I thought my heart would burst right out of my chest.

"You are the girls that live with Denzil – oui? Denzil is my life saver. I should have died if it was not for Denzil. He is a fine man and very brave. They were all brave – those men in their little ships. They even took on board dogs retreating from Belgium and France."

"Yes, Denzil did tell us. Actually it took a while for Denzil to tell us anything, Henri. He needed lots of rest when he got home to Padstow."

Sister walked towards us carrying a tray.

"Henri – time for your medication and a nice cool drink of lemonade. One each for you girls, too. Polly dear, can you come with me now – two more patients have just arrived!"

"I will see you again, Polly – oui?"

"Yes, of course." I said, walking away with a backward glance. Vera was sitting at Henri's feet, chatting away. I felt a little left out.

Having finished my work, I found Vera and Henri were sitting in the same place I had left them.

"Hello Polly – nice to have you join us. Have you been nursing some lucky chap?"

"Well, changed his dressing. Sister watched me and said I did a good job. What have you two been talking about?"

I hoped I didn't sound too jealous.

"Vera has been telling me all about herself, and me too. Now I need to know all about you, Polly."

I'm sure I blushed.

"We have to get back to help with supper. Come along, Vera and you too, Lucky."

"Must we?" moaned Vera.

"Come again soon, girls – please." Henri was looking at me when he spoke.

"He's lovely, Polly," gushed Vera.

"Well, I could tell you were smitten, Vera!"

"Don't tease, Polly. He likes you too."

"Come on Vera, we have work to do at home."

Vera reached for my hand as we waved goodbye to Henri.

"Really Vera, I think we are a little old to be holding hands," I said, far too sharply.

"Ooo – listen to you, Miss High and Mighty!"

Chapter Twenty-Six

"You're shuffling, Polly!"

"I can't sleep, Vera."

"What's up, Pol?" Vera snuggled down beside me in our bed.

"I was horrible to you, Vera – I'm sorry. I was jealous – you know – about you and Henri."

"Don't be daft, Pol. He does like you too, you know. You're much cleverer than me anyway!"

My letter from Auntie this morning was full of news about cousin Laura coming to stay with her from London, and then planning to go up to Scarborough to stay with friends.

"But they're safe, Polly – your Auntie and her cousin. It's lovely that they have each other for company. Shame they couldn't come here."

I shot a look at Ma across the table.

"But it's no good, Polly dear – all the trains are being used to transport the troops."

I suddenly felt very homesick.

Vera interrupted our chat by tearing into the kitchen, followed close behind by Lucky.

"There was another plane flying low over the rise, Ma – gave me and Lucky a fright. There seem to be so many now, Ma, toing and froing across the bay, and lots of ships too. Are they the ones carrying food?"

"I expect so, darling."

Ma didn't seem to want to talk any more, but delved deep into the sink to wash some beans.

"You off up to Gull House again this evening, girls?"

"What do you think, Vera – shall we just call and see Henri and take Lucky? Lucky needs her evening run, doesn't she, Ma?"

"Good idea, you two – take that rascal away from under my feet."

We found Henri outside, gazing across the bay. He seemed pleased to see us.

"Polly, Vera and Lucky, how lovely to see you." Henri grinned, leaning down to pet Lucky.

"Anything we can do for you, Henri?" I asked.

"Well, a strange request maybe, but I wondered if you could find a small paintbrush and, of course, one or two paints. Is this possible?"

Vera looked at me and shrugged.

"We can't promise but we will try. I will speak to Denzil."

"Thank you, Polly. The light, here in Cornwall, is so beautiful – like none I have seen before. I painted a lot at home."

"How are you, Henri?"

We both sat at his feet and Lucky settled down too, her head tucked between her paws.

"A little pain but not too much. Sister makes me walk a little with my crutches, and has said in a while I should manage with one. Thank you for asking. I have something to tell you, Polly and Vera."

Oh, oh, I thought, he's going away now he's getting better.

"I sit here a lot, in this place under the tree, and last evening I heard a beautiful sound – singing sound – it came from the sea."

"It was her, Henri – the Siren I told you about."

I couldn't believe Vera had told him about the Siren when Denzil had said it was just mine water running under ground.

"It was beautiful, Vera, but I wondered if it could be a silkie. My mother used to tell me Irish folk tales and one was about the seals who could turn themselves into silkies – beautiful maidens with lovely voices. But maybe it was the medicine the doctor gives me for pain. Ah – all nonsense perhaps. Anyway, I would love to paint this place here by the sea."

"Well," said Denzil, "I might have one or two small brushes, Vera, that I use to touch up Morwenna, but I don't have any proper paints for the lad. I'll ask our neighbour – her George used to do some messing about with paints, before he joined up. In fact, why don't you two go and see her, Vera? She's missing the lad something dreadful – hasn't heard a word from the Ministry and has no idea where he is, poor soul. She lives at the end of the quay, near the pub called The Lobster Pot."

Vera knocked gently on the red door and, after a few seconds, it was cautiously opened by a tiny lady. We couldn't remember having seen her before in Padstow.

"Yes, midears – what can I do for you?"

"I'm Vera, Missus, and this is Polly. We live with Ma and Denzil - we're evacuees."

"Come in, do, darlin's – come in – how lovely to meet you. I 'ave a problem with mi feet so I don't get out much, but Ma and Denzil are always on the lookout for me. Come in, do.

"Ma talks a lot about you and the two boys. She's really enjoying having you all to stay. My lad is missing in France – 'aven't eard a word. Denzil said not to give up hope, though. Now what can I do for you?"

"We have a friend, Missus, a French boy – one of those rescued at Dunkirk by Denzil." I let Vera carry on with the story about Henri.

"Well, that's a wonderful thing that he is here in Cornwall and recovering – poor boy. Is he very young?"

"Sixteen, we think – he lied about his age to join up in France."

"Well, I think I can help him - with the paints, that is. George loved to paint. I'm sure my lad wouldn't mind if your Henri used them – no good sitting in a box." The corner of her apron was raised to dash away a tear.

We left with arms full of paper, paints and brushes, telling Nellie, as she wanted to be called, "Henri is going to be so pleased." I said this, squeezing Vera's arms.

The weekend couldn't come soon enough.

Chapter Twenty-Seven

I went to Gull House on Saturday to help the nurses and took the paints with me. Vera was busy bottling fruit with Ma, and didn't mind me going alone to see Henri.

"These are wonderful, Polly. I will write a note to the lady to thank her," he said, beaming.

I finished helping Sister, collected Henri's thank-you note and returned to Quay Cottage, hungry for the mushroom pie Ma had promised for tea.

And then there was a development. Henri was told he was well enough to leave Gull House. Where would he go from there, we wondered.

"What will he do, Pol? He can't manage on his own and he can't return to France." Vera agonized.

Denzil, as always, had a solution.

"Why don't I speak to Nellie and ask her if she would care to house Henri, for the time being anyway? They would be company for one another, and Ma and I can keep an eye on them both. The Ministry would have to approve, of course, and they would give Nellie some financial support whilst he is with her."

Both Nellie and Henri were delighted at the prospect of staying together and within days the Ministry, doctors and all concerned approved the move. Henri could not be repatriated to France due to his extensive injuries. Needless to say, Vera and I were thrilled at the prospect of him being close by. Even Billy and Jack were excited. A real French boy to chat to, instead of two lasses!

And so began another chapter in our lives in Padstow.

From our bedroom window I watched Henri sitting on the quay with paint brushes and paints alongside a basket. He would be joined by Lucky when she wasn't shadowing Denzil.

Henri's blue hospital suit had been returned to Gull House, and was replaced ("just for the time being, mind," said Nellie) by clothes left behind by George. Henri promised not to get paint splashed on them. He looked every bit the artist in his big white shirt.

"Doesn't talk about his Ma and Pa," Nellie told me, "but he will when he's ready, Polly".

Nellie enjoyed taking care of Henri. She didn't mind changing his dressings one bit, and he was managing to move around her cottage on two crutches. Soon Henri would return to hospital to have something called a prosthesis fitted to his lower limb. Denzil had already offered to drive him to Plymouth, provided he could get the precious petrol.

I had watched Henri painting the view across the quay to Rock a few days earlier, and asked if he had completed it.

"Indeed yes, Polly, and I would like to give the painting of Rock to Denzil as a thank-you for the paints and brushes. Nellie has one or two of my sketches. She has been so very kind to me."

"Denzil will love your painting, Henri, especially of Rock. Rock is where Denzil and Ma's little girl Morwenna is buried. She died when she was only four." I said softly.

Henri turned a shocked face to mine.

"That is terrible, Polly. Poor Denzil and Ma. I wish there was some way I could let Papa know that I am safe. If, indeed, he is alive."

I was lost for words.

And so the days drifted on. Everyone talked about the rationing. Meat was rationed, bacon, butter and sugar, but somehow Ma managed to fill us up. We were growing our own vegetables of course, and dear Bernard was still able to get us the odd rabbit or hare from up at Gull House. But Ma missed the endless cups of tea which she and Denzil had been used to, because even tea was rationed too. Vera, Billy, Jack and I were quite happy with water. I don't think Billy and Jack had ever drunk anything else back home in Leeds.

The old wireless was on permanently now, spluttering away. Ma enjoyed Workers Playtime, but more than anything she loved to sing along.

"Cheers me up, girls," said Ma, waltzing round the kitchen table followed by Lucky.

At the beginning of June, just when Cornwall was dressed in vibrant colours, the hills around Padstow full of yellows and blue, sitting under a jewel-blue sky, things began to take on a more serious tone. The old wireless hinted at a build-up of German interest in invading our country. If the wireless was on when we walked into the kitchen, Ma would promptly switch it off.

"Don't need to know that nonsense, girls." And she would fiddle with the knob until she found some music.

The war had seemed so far away until now, except for the aircraft and the ships patrolling the Atlantic west of us.

Now, we realized, lovely Cornwall was involved in the fight and the previously carefree atmosphere was changing rapidly.

Chapter Twenty-Eight

Collecting a rabbit one day, Bernard told us some of the more seriously injured had been moved to the ground floor of Gull House, including the basement. Upstairs windows were now permanently blacked out. All the Padstow cottages had had their blackout curtains up for some time. We children were told we must be home before dark. Even Lucky seemed to sense a change, and ran for cover under the kitchen table when she heard approaching aircraft or any noise which she didn't recognise.

Ma suggested we limit our visits to Gull House, and so I was only able to help Sister on Sunday after Chapel.

Denzil said the Padstow lifeboat was on permanent standby in case of ditchings in the sea off the beaches, and the radar station on the cliff above Rock was manned 24 hours a day now.

Nellie and Henri sat together on the quay, contentedly chatting whilst Henri painted. Sitting with the two, Vera and I took some ginger beer which Ma had made. Not real beer but ginger beer. Ma had grown the ginger herself. There was no end to her culinary talent. We had scarcely missed all the rationed food. We watched Henri deftly painting the scene before him, little boats bobbing about, but tied up when not working, Denzil in the distance tending to Morwenna, the sun going down over Rock and, all the time, Nellie looking on admiringly.

Something caught my attention. With Henri's shirt sleeve rolled up so as not to get paint splashes on it, I saw a mark, a birthmark perhaps, on Henri's forearm.

I nudged Vera and whispered "Do you see it, Vera – it's just like a fish – on Henri's arm? Perhaps he painted it on himself."

"Go on – never," said Vera, peering closer over Henri's shoulder.

"I know what you are looking at, girls." Henri turned and smiled. "It's my present from Papa."

"What do you mean?"

"It's a birthmark. Papa has an identical mole on his other arm. It looks like a seal or a silkie – oui, or maybe a mermaid!"

"Oh, I see it now – look, Vera – there's the tail. It's beautiful." We both drew closer, marvelling at the fish swimming up Henri's arm.

"Well I never!" said Nellie, peering over her spectacles at the strange creature.

"Time you went home, girls, and us too, Henri. The sun will drop like a stone soon, and we must get back to the cottage before blackout."

"Come on, Lucky – tea time." Vera called to the pup, who yawned, stretched and tore up the quay to the cottage.

"Henri doesn't seem to be bothered about the aircraft and news on the wireless. Does Nellie have a wireless, Pol?"

"Not sure, but it's pretty obvious that Padstow is on alert or something. Anyway, we are better off here in Padstow than the poor people in the big cities. I'm so pleased Auntie and her cousin have moved out of Leeds and gone to Scarborough."

"I hope Mam and Dad and our Lionel are OK. They've got the air-raid shelter, anyway."

I changed the subject quickly. Vera was looking anxious again.

"I can smell something delicious even from here, Vera," and I grabbed Vera's arm, hurrying her along.

We could hear Ma's hens clucking as we drew closer to the cottage and that cheered us.

Chapter Twenty-Nine

Denzil told us Henri's doctor decided he was fit enough, and his wound healed enough, to go to Plymouth to be fitted with his prosthesis and so he was making plans to take him. "The news isn't good, girls, so I need to set off and come home by dusk."

Nellie came with us to see Denzil and Henri off. She gave him a hug and pushed a parcel into his arms.

"Musn't leave those paints behind, mi 'andsome, they will help take your mind off – well – your mind off the hospital smells."

Henri looked deeply moved, and lingered over his farewell embrace.

We stood back, holding Lucky, who was not too happy about being left behind.

"See you soon Henri, we'll take care of Nellie!" said Ma. The old truck Denzil had borrowed rattled down the hill as we continued to wave until it was out of sight.

"Come on, Vera, work to do."

"We'll miss Henri, won't we, Pol?" Vera sniffed.

"He will come back Vera, he promised." I answered uncertainly.

Vera and I were still at Padstow School. We had no idea when it would be possible to start at Newquay High. Everything seemed to have come to a standstill, and there was a dreadful air of uncertainty. Ma tried her best to keep us busy and, therefore, to lift our spirits.

"Boys, you can give Morwenna a good clean for Denzil whilst he's gone. I expect he'll be back as soon as he has settled Henri at the hospital. Must take advantage of this lovely weather. Girls, we can clean out the hen house and do some more bottling. After that we'll take Nellie to Newquay on the bus and have a picnic."

The mood at Quay Cottage had changed, thanks to Ma.

Nellie was a bit overwhelmed at the prospect of a bus ride to Newquay.

"But mi feet are terrible, Ma – not sure I'll manage to walk very far."

"You won't need to, Nellie. My friend lives right by the bus stop close to the beach. She will be more than happy to let you sit in her garden, and I'll take the girls for a bit of crabbing on the beach. You will be able to see us all the time, Nellie. We'll have a picnic and get the 3 o'clock bus home. Do you good, Nellie, I promise."

The boys were happy to stay home with Lucky and finish off their swabbing of Morwenna. And we had promised to bring them back a fresh crab for tea, and cockles.

There were the ever-present aircraft flying overhead but we barely noticed them, Vera and I, as we delved into the rock pools looking for crabs, with Nellie sitting above us waving.

On the return bus ride, contentedly nibbling our Newquay rock and Nellie looking a bit tired but with rosy cheeks from the kind sun, we marvelled once more at our good fortune to be here, in Cornwall, with Ma and Denzil.

"Makes me feel a bit sad Mam and Dad and our Lionel are not here to share this, Polly." Vera sat close, tucking her arm in mine.

"I know, Vera, I feel the same, but we are here because our families wanted us to be safe – so we must just thank our lucky stars we ended up with Ma and Denzil. Don't forget it wasn't always good, not at the beginning when you and the boys were shut up at Gull House with that dreadful housekeeper. It hasn't always been plain sailing, as Denzil would say!"

"Do you think we'll win the war, Pol?" Now Vera was looking anxious.

"Of course, silly." I hugged her close and felt her relax.

"You've soon gone through that rock already, Pol!" And now she giggled.

Chapter Thirty

July arrived hot and humid. Flaming June had passed with an increase in tension.

Denzil was no longer interested in keeping any news from the four of us, despite Ma turning the wireless off whenever we came into the kitchen.

Denzil told us Germany was trying to eliminate the RAF both in the air and on the ground. Operating from airfields in France and Belgium, the Luftwaffe began their onslaught directed at shipping and channel ports. The intention, Denzil said, was not only to sink ships but to draw the RAF into combat and wear down its strength.

Denzil was kept busy manning the radar station on Rock, and Brian's dad and his crews manned the lifeboat twenty-four hours a day. Miraculously there had been no ditched aircraft at sea, so far anyway.

Vera hadn't been sleeping well and sometimes, in the morning, I would find her tucked into her blanket with a pillow on the floor beside our bed. But I didn't tell Ma.

"What are you doing on the floor, Vera?" I asked gently.

"I feel safer down here, Pol."

"Come in with me silly, and cuddle up, I'm cold without you beside me."

Not true really as the nights were hot and sticky.

"Even Lucky hides under Ma's bed at night, Polly."

Whenever Denzil was at home, however, he was cheerful and comforting.

"Our lads will see them off, darlings, don't fret. The boys are flying all the hours God sends, and I'll bet they're enjoying the dog fights too."

"What do you mean 'dog fights', Denzil?" Vera asked looking alarmed.

"You know, skirmishes, Vera – zooming around the skies in their Spitfires trying to shoot down the Germans in their Messerschmitts. Most of the aircrew are very young, Vera, not much older than you and Polly. Anyway – one way or another - I have to get down to Plymouth to collect Henri this week. Looks like some bad weather is on the way for a change, and that will put paid to some of the Luftwaffe's fun!"

"Henri coming back, Denzil – what wonderful news." We beamed at one another, Vera and I.

"Can we go and tell Nellie, please Denzil?" Vera asked.

"Of course, Vera. We need to check up on Nellie anyway, girls. She will be wondering about all the air activity over at St Eval. You do know, girls, don't you, that the boys rely on St Eval Church's high tower to guide them to the airfield and back home. There are men up the tower 24 hours a day manning the wirelesses. Somebody wanted to dismantle the tower but the pilots said it was a valuable landmark."

"You did tell us, Denzil. You said what an interesting history St Eval Church had. Let's hope it doesn't get damaged," I said, turning to Vera.

"Well, must be off, girls – look after Ma for me, I'll be back as soon as possible. Keep an eye on the pup, girls – I can't take her with me this time."

We waved Denzil off from the cottage door. Another friend who needed a run to Plymouth was taking Denzil, and the return journey with Henri would be by Red Cross ambulance. Denzil said the doctor at Gull House was expecting four more injured.

Lucky came to Nellie's cottage with us to tell her the good news.

"Oh lovely – I'll do some baking, girls. Do you think your hens would give me a couple of eggs?"

"Nellie, have you been alright? There have been so many aircraft and things – you're not frightened, are you?" I asked.

"Goodness no, but it will be nice to have Henri for company again."

Denzil arrived back just after dark, having taken Henri up to Gull House to see the doctor. Matron took in the other injured men from the ambulance.

"He's fine, girls, but needs some rest now. You will be able to go up and see him in a day or two. I will tell Nellie in the morning. Now off to sleep – I'm dead beat," said Denzil, climbing the stairs.

Chapter Thirty-One

We could barely contain ourselves, Vera and I, at the thought of seeing Henri again. How would he look? Would he have proper clothes on with trousers over his 'tin leg', as he liked to call it, or would he be wearing a blue suit like the other casualties from Gull House?

We went to Chapel with Denzil, Ma and the boys and then raced up the cliff path with Lucky tearing ahead. She knew she would be seeing Henri, we were sure.

A plane flew low over us on its return to St Eval airfield. We had almost got used to the activity overhead. The war was on our doorstep now but Padstow seemed unchanged. There had been some damage, Denzil said, to the airstrip and even some buildings but the church, with its splendid tower, was unscathed. We had seen Hawker Hurricanes, Bristol Blenheim fighters as well, of course, as the Supermarine Spitfires. We had all become expert 'plane spotters'.

During one afternoon a JU88 dropped eight bombs causing some damage, but it was chased off by two Spitfires.

Billy and Jack still seemed more interested in the boats whereas we thought, Vera and I, that they would both be smitten with flying.

Arriving at Gull House we looked for Matron to find out where Henri was.

"Girls, come in quickly, there is too much flying going on. Are you sure Denzil is happy that you climb the cliff path?"

"Well he was with the lifeboat, Matron, but he does know we were coming to see Henri. Is it alright that we brought Lucky?"

"Of course, girls. Henri will be pleased to see all of you," and she reached down to rub Lucky's head.

We went into a different part of the house, away from the wards and Henri was in the middle of a session of physiotherapy which was the name the nurses gave to the exercises Henri would need to do to get used to his new 'tin leg'.

"My dear friends and Lucky! Be a good pup and don't jump up, Lucky, or you might break my new leg." Henri grinned. But Lucky lay down to watch Henri walk towards us. He didn't need crutches at all.

"Henri, you look wonderful," I said.

"Doesn't he, Vera! You are walking so well," said the physiotherapist.

"All thanks to everyone who has taken care of me. Everyone at the Plymouth hospital treated me with much kindness and there were many injured to take care of. We brought some back here, girls, in the ambulance but I didn't see much of them. Anyway, how are you?"

Henri sat down for a rest and his nurse left the room.

"It's been quite hectic here, Henri, with a massive increase in the flying but we feel quite safe with Denzil around. Well, actually, Vera is a bit nervous."

I looked across at Vera but she didn't sniff or scowl. I just wanted to draw her into our conversation.

"Just a bit, Henri. The aircraft make such a terrible din," said Vera.

"Din? – what is din, Vera?"

And we laughed together feeling elated and just pleased. Henri was back with us.

"Girls!" said Matron coming into the room, "It's time for Henri to rest now."

"Au revoir, my dear friends" said Henri. "Come back soon." And Henri waved and patted Lucky on his way out.

Chapter Thirty-Two

Before leaving Gull House I arranged to return at the weekend to work. Vera said she wanted to come too but might have to help Ma.

It proved difficult settling in to any kind of normality at the cottage. So much seemed to have taken our attention away from chores, study, walking Lucky and helping Ma and Nellie. The wireless was on permanently once more, and the Battle of Britain was in full swing.

When I arrived back at Gull House quite a lot of the beds had been put into a basement ward. This was for the seriously injured. The rest of the patients who could walk were scattered throughout the lower rooms of the house. I helped to re-arrange beds and make them up with bedding. Halfway through my work I hadn't yet had a chance to see Henri. But then, during my break time, Sister found me and, taking my hand, led me through the house.

"What is it Sister, where are we going?" I asked, still munching my toast.

"You need to see Henri, Polly – he has some exciting news, my love – finish your toast quickly. I have to get back to work."

We went to the physio ward where Henri greeted me, face alight with excitement, tottering along without his crutches.

"Polly – oh Polly – it is magnifique, it is a miracle, dear friend. Quickly, come with me."

We left the physio ward and made our way to the next floor above. I helped Henri climb the stairs, thankfully only a few, and into a room with just a few patients in beds and some in chairs.

"Come, come follow me, Polly, I wish to show you something but you must be very quiet."

I was led to one of the beds. The patient lay, his face almost completely swathed in bandages.

"See, Polly – his arm - do you see the mark?" Henri drew me closer to the bedside.

"What do you see, ma chère?"

"Oh Henri – its – it's a birthmark – it's a fish exactly like the one you have."

And Henri raised his shirt sleeve to show me, once more, the dolphin-like creature.

"This is my Papa, Polly – I am sure, but what do I do – should I ask Matron if he has identification?" Henri pleaded.

"Of course, you must ask Matron and the doctors and we will go find her right now."

We made our way back to the main hall. I could feel Henri shaking with emotion as he painstakingly walked beside me.

"Are you sure, Henri?" Matron asked.

"Oui Matron – I just know it is Papa, please help me."

Henri told Matron and the doctor who joined us about the birthmark he shared with his father.

The patient was French and was one of those struggling through the water at Dunkirk to reach the safety of the little ships. He had identification also. He was a civilian and had been hiding in a neighbour's farm when the invasion began. Some of the detail he could not remember but he kept repeating that he had to find his son – a young soldier. There was no wife – she had died several years ago. His injuries were not serious but his face had burns from burning oil.

"Polly dear, will you leave us for the moment. The doctors will need to talk with Henri in some detail."

"Of course, Matron," I replied to her request.

"I will see you soon, Henri, I promise. Would you rather I didn't tell Denzil and Ma, and of course Vera, about this news until you are certain?"

"I am certain, Polly, and so you can tell the whole of Padstow about this miracle. I have found Papa – I have found my beloved Papa!" Henri put one free arm around my shoulder and kissed me on both cheeks.

"I'm not sure whether I should tell Vera that!"

Chapter Thirty-Three

Climbing down the cliff path to Quay Cottage I could scarcely take in Henri's news. Henri might have found the only family he has. It was a miracle but somehow it would change everything. Nothing would be the same for us. We would remain friends of course, but now Henri might leave with his father.

Ma was cleaning out the hen coop when I arrived back. I decided to wait until we were all together before telling them.

"Polly – sit down darling – your supper will go cold. Boys, have you washed your hands?"

"Where's Denzil, Ma?" I asked.

"Oh, he will be here any time, Polly. I think he might have taken Lucky for a short walk. She doesn't like to go too far at the moment, too much noise from the aircraft."

"You're a bit quiet, Polly." Vera nudged me.

"I'm fine – really. I worked hard at Gull House. Almost didn't have time for a break."

"Did you see Henri, Pol?"

"Yes Vera, I did. Tell you about him later."

When Denzil joined us, and Ma sat still for a moment I told them the news about Henri's Papa.

"But that's wonderful!" Ma exclaimed.

"In the middle of all this to-do – planes and things – we have some good news at last. Bless the dear boy. If it is him then it is another miracle, girls."

We had never known Denzil lost for words, but he was. And we saw him wipe a tear from his good eye.

"And the two of them shared the same ambulance all the way from Plymouth and never knew. He must have been in the hospital when Henri had his new leg fitted as well. Saints preserve us, Ma."

Denzil told Nellie and so there was more dabbing of eyes and sniffs of delight.

"I'm sure you will be meeting Henri's Papa soon, Nellie, but we must wait a while longer, I'm afraid."

"I can wait, Denzil. Spent my life waiting for men, I have."

And Nellie made more cake – just in case.

Chapter Thirty-Four

Just as expected, our lives did change quite a lot over the following months.

The Battle of Britain was in full swing and St Eval was extremely busy throughout August with direct hits damaging three Blenheims, but Hurricanes managed to shoot down two German aircraft.

Gull House remained unscathed and Padstow was little changed.

Quay Cottage was our sanctuary; Ma tending her hens, the boys helping Denzil much of the time, and Vera and I visiting Henri and his Papa who had moved in with Nellie, whilst "all the paperwork was completed." said Henri. It was quite possible the two would be able to stay.

Henri still found time to paint on the quayside during quiet periods, this time with his Papa sitting beside him, and occasionally visited by Lucky when the aircraft weren't too noisy.

"It is good to know Auntie is happy in Scarborough with her cousin and you know, Vera, that your Mam, Dad and Lionel are safe."

"Do you think we will still be able to go to High School, Polly?" asked Vera.

"I'm not sure, Vera, but going to lessons at Padstow school is fine for the time being. We'll see how things are in September when we should be starting. We've got plenty to keep us busy though, and they still want our help at Gull House."

"I do miss Mam and Dad and our Lionel, Polly. I wonder when I will be able to see them." Vera looked sad.

"What can I say, Vera? I miss Auntie and Trouble but everything depends on – well – so much. I do know though that they are very relieved that we are here in Cornwall."

"We've had so many lovely adventures, Pol. Finding the seal, finding Lucky – of course, getting Denzil back from Dunkirk and meeting Henri. Being with Henri when he found his Papa. We have been lucky, Pol, haven't we?"

"We certainly have, and I'm sure the adventures haven't ended. Anyway, we have Nellie to look after – her son is still missing, and Ma says we can go and visit Mrs Cadel sometime – she must be missing Gull House. After all, it is really her house and the Ministry are only borrowing it."

"I would like a walk to Siren's Cave to see if I can hear her Pol."

"Now Vera, we've told you, the sound you heard when you got stuck in the mine was water underneath. But I will go with you and we can look for crabs. Lucky would enjoy that."

"We can take Henri and his Papa with us, and see if Henri can hear the Siren, or silkie as he called her." Vera beamed.

We celebrated my birthday on 3rd September and a short time later the Battle of Britain reached a climax.

Walking back from the beach and into dear old Quay Cottage we joined Ma, Denzil and the boys around the crackling old wireless.

Mr Winston Churchill was making a speech. It was the 10th September.

"One of the decisive battles of the war has reached its climax. The gratitude of every home in our island, in our Empire and, indeed throughout the world, goes out to the British airmen who, undaunted by odds, unwearied in their constant challenge and mortal danger, are turning the tide of World War by their prowess and by their devotion. Never in the field of human conflict was so much owed by so many to so few."

"Have we won the war, Denzil?" asked Billy.

"Not quite, Billy. We have some way to go yet, but I think we can safely say that Padstow is safe, and so are you, son," and Denzil ruffled Billy's hair.

"Come on, lads. We need to get Morwenna ready to do a big fish tonight. Come on Lucky – you can come too."

Vera and I followed Denzil, Billy and Jack to do some crabbing and, who knows, we might just hear the Siren in her cave.

THE END

Epilogue

By January 1940 almost sixty percent of evacuees had returned to their homes.

However, a second evacuation effort was started after the Germans had taken over most of France. From June 13th to June 18th 1940 around 100,000 children were evacuated (in many cases re-evacuated).

The Blitz (heavy German bombing of industrial areas) followed the Battle of Britain, but by the end of 1941, city centres, especially London, became safer.

From June 1944, the Germans attacked again by firing V1 rockets on Britain, followed later by V2 ballistic missiles. One million women, children, elderly and disabled people were evacuated from London. This new way of attacking Britain from the air carried on until the end of the war in Europe in May 1945

World War II ended in September 1945. However, evacuation did not officially end until March 1946 when it was felt that Britain mainland was no longer under threat. Surprisingly, even six months after the war ended there were still 5,200 evacuees living in rural areas with their host families.

Most evacuees kept in touch with their host families long after the war had ended.